ALSO BY ROBERTA COLE

Caregiving from the Heart: tales of inspiration
Elders Academy Press

READING MY MIND

A Collection of Essays

ROBERTA COLE

iUniverse, Inc.

Bloomington

Reading My Mind
A Collection of Essays

Copyright © 2012 Roberta Cole

iUniverse books may be ordered through booksellers or by contacting:

iUniverse
1663 Liberty Drive
Bloomington, IN 47403
www.iuniverse.com
1-800-Authors (1-800-288-4677)

ISBN: 978-1-4620-5580-7 (sc)
ISBN: 978-1-4620-5582-1 (hc)
ISBN: 978-1-4620-5581-4 (e)

Printed in the United States of America

iUniverse rev. date: 2/15/2012

Front Cover Design by John Kisch
Rhinebeck, New York

For Jeff
My mind reader for all time

The point is to make as much world as possible in whatever small clearing is allotted one.
—Vivian Gornick, *Fierce Attachments*

Contents

Introduction

One day, smack in the middle of grown-up life, I stopped dead in my tracks and found myself pretty close to where I had started. I was seven again, standing on the edge of a curb on the corner of New York's Riverside Drive with my dad. The daydream felt as if I were on a carousel ride that spins effortlessly around, exposing sights along the way, until ultimately it stops, providing an opportunity to climb off the horse. Like the carousel ride, I needed the motion to stop so I could pause and try to make sense of a world that was spinning endlessly around. That's when my stories started to tell themselves; it was the birth of this essay collection.

Some of the pieces in this book were previously published in another form and have been revised to reflect more current details. Others, previously unpublished, remain as they were initially conceived even though some specifics may have been changed. These pages reflect the latitude and longitude of a life—from rituals of the daily grind and a love of the Golden State to the torment of losing a friend, from being seduced into retirement to watching my daughter stand triumphant under the steamy Louisiana sun to receive her law degree. These essays simply follow the trajectory of a restless mind.

This collection is divided into visits with people who have touched me, places that have mattered, and things that have caught my attention. The world has undergone a sea change, culturally and socially, since I have come of age. Much of the time these days, I find myself running to stay in place. Perhaps you do as well. Peeping through the keyhole of experience is not always a comfortable thing to do, but it does afford an opportunity to see whatever is there head-on. It is not my intention, through these essays, to arrive at any destination. It is my intention only to observe the stops along the way.

All any of us can do on this great journey is to travel light, to keep an open mind and heart, and to watch and listen intently. I hope you, the reader, will enjoy meandering along with me.

PEOPLE

You gradually struggle less and less for an
idea and more and more for specific people.
In the end, it is the reality of personal
relationship that saves everything.
—Thomas Merton

RIVERSIDE DRIVE

"There goes another Pontiac, Daddy. Is it black or dark blue?"

"I call it blue," he said.

"What color car would you get, Daddy? Could we get one?"

"We don't need a car in the city. But why don't we rent one and go for a drive in the country next weekend?"

I looked back with glee as he gently ushered me away from the curb, back to the safety of the bench.

It was late spring that night we sat on the drive. I was seven, maybe eight. We'd gone there many times before. Riverside Drive stretches along the perimeter of Manhattan's western urban oasis, Riverside Park. My childhood was spent on the fourteenth floor of one of the prewar fortresses lining the other side of the park.

With one small hand clasped in my dad's, keeping the other free to manage a tower of strawberry icicles dripping onto a cone of sugar, we cataloged the traffic as it went by. Those evenings usually ended with the promise of a day outside the city. I knew just how it would go. We would glide along the West Side Highway, slowly and deliberately heading nowhere. My mother would be there too, but my guess was that this was not her idea of recreation. Upon arriving in some town far enough north of Westchester to be considered "the country," we'd disembark and walk slowly through the village streets, our arms twisted around each other to enclose us from the rest of the world. Before leaving, I was always able to coax them into buying some trinket to commemorate the day. It rarely lasted through the trip home, but the thought of it lasted much longer and continues to play a sweet refrain in my reverie of all that has been lost. On the ride home, with the sweet orange overhead pouring its juice into the twilight air and my thighs clinging to the moist vinyl upholstery, I would lay my head against a crevice of the car and let the rocking motion seduce me to sleep.

My childhood was mostly uneventful: a repetition of tender mercies and bewildering challenges. It was filled with the agonies of figuring out just how much like real life my life was, while keeping current with pop tunes, skirt length, and, whenever possible, my homework. My parents captivated me. My father had Clark Gable looks but seemed to negate the macho stereotype of his generation. There was a complexity about him at the same time that he appeared relaxed and serene. He had no patience for artifice. He screamed at injustice, cried at songs, and seemed not to say much at all to those he considered "strangers"—that is, anyone who was not part of his inner circle. From time to time, his passion caught fire. When he hugged me, it was with a gusto seen only in Italian opera—"Mack, you'll hurt her," my mother would say. She was right. He spoiled it for me; I have never been hugged that way again.

Sometimes I had trouble making sense of his behavior. On Saturday mornings, I would observe a curious ritual: he would stand by the window of our large living room, busily arranging the draperies to allow a peek of golden light to cast a shadow on an otherwise somber interior. Outside, the craggy gray facade of the building across the courtyard would become visible. When he did this, it was with the kind of determination that suggested that he had no choice. It drove my mother crazy. "How will you get them back in place?" She would ask with concern. Every Monday morning they were back in place.

It seemed as simple as his needing to let some light in. As I grew older, I understood that need and wondered how different it would have been had music or literature been his chosen work rather than becoming a physician. Suppose his hands had waved wildly to Beethoven instead of neatly adjudicating medical claims at the Veterans Administration after he left private practice? My mother, on the other hand, had none of his intensity. She was governed by good common sense and was well adjusted to a fault. Her only excess was a boundless capacity for kindness. Unlike my father, my mother did not have flamboyant good looks, and I certainly didn't get the impression that she thought so. The only awareness of her ability to attract that I ever observed was her trip on board a ship to the Panama Canal. In a photograph proudly displayed in her bedroom, she was outfitted in shorts and a halter. She surely had been told that the costume flattered her, even made her look beautiful. But I never really saw her as beautiful—that is, until I learned something about life.

I was just shy of fourteen when a virulent cancer took hold of my father's body. My father the physician became my father the patient. I remember when my mother told me the news, straight and direct at a back table in Schrafft's with only a butterscotch almond sundae to cushion the blow. I kept looking for signs, for something to tell me where we really stood. There were none—just one crumpled tissue in my mother's clenched fist. I had been watching my father. In the past, he would approach me with his black bag at the sign of any minor symptom. I worked hard to conceal evidence that would curtail my adolescent escapades. Suddenly, a persistent cough could go easily unnoticed. That black bag was needed to measure my father's steady decline. The more I witnessed the signs of his deterioration, the more I chattered on the phone. Shakespeare would have to wait. My grades fell as his white count fluctuated. Slow walks were taken from his bedroom to the dinette. Very slow walks. Grand and gracious hand-me-downs from my grandmother's lavish West End Avenue apartment were moved aside to make room for the furnishings of illness. My mother struggled to concoct some form of edible material that would heal. Nothing helped. Everything changed. The starched taffeta fabric my mother's deft hands had been slated to turn into the prom dress to turn heads lay neglected on the closet floor. There was work to do, and it wasn't pretty. Periods of restored hope were punctuated by bursts of agony. At night, I would pull my trusted blanket over my delicately developing body and wonder where I would be when the end came. Would I be taking a final or kissing my first boyfriend?

When the end came, I knew. My mother's face spoke sadly: there would be no more evenings on the drive. And so we started, ever so slowly, to pick up the pieces and to reinvent ourselves. My mother knew a new life beckoned, away from the dreary days of waiting in the cavernous old apartment. We moved to Queens—the Queens of tennis championships, the Queens of the World's Fair, but not the Queens of my mother. It was a foreign land to her. We might as well have gone to outer Mongolia. My new school was majestic and welcoming at the end of a leafy road adorned with low houses, far from Riverside Drive. Great halls of glitz lined the boulevards—places where it was possible to hold events honoring life's milestones that were elaborate enough to rival a presidential inauguration for the price of a package deal. "Where are we?" She used to say. Some of my classes in Queens were as big as my entire grade in the private school I had left. All the rules had changed.

My mother took a job at Bergdorf Goodman, an emporium of good taste to match her own, and there she flourished—first as a salesperson and later as manager of a high-end French fashion boutique. I can't remember how many times I visited her there, only to be presented to the legion of widows and divorcées working at various outposts in the store. "Meet my Roberta," she would say, beaming with pride. It seemed a new kind of self-expression had begun to define her existence.

"I need a passport right away," was the cry on the other end of the phone one Sunday morning. "They're sending me to Paris." Or was it paradise? Her voice sure sounded like it was. Breathless excitement was not something I witnessed very often in my mother's life. But I heard it that day, and I filled with joy at the thought that this dear soul had been recognized by the very population that commanded her attention. Dressing the grand dames, being part of a world of beauty and elegance, and knowing that she was admired and respected by her colleagues gave her great satisfaction. And it wasn't merely about a man, as it was for so many of her generation. No, she wasn't interested in spending her time "washing some old buzzard's socks."

Too bad it all came so late. My mother continued to work until her legs gave out. Nearly eight decades on this earth were enough to make the case for an ottoman and some pampering. And so a new chapter began. It was a time to step back into the role she knew best—the role of nurturer. My daughter and I were the beneficiaries. She was a mainstay in our home. From my daughter's earliest discordant cries of colic that had us bouncing off the walls to the birthday parties with too much cake and too many disappearing rabbits, Grandma was there. She picked up, dropped off, and stayed the course when we were so tired we were near delirium. And we all grew older. And then there were times when we got our signals crossed, when appointments were missed, when urgent staccato messages were left on my answering machine. And then there was that day. We had planned to meet at our favorite local watering hole. Walking had become such a struggle for my mother that I stationed myself close to the corner to help her from the bus to the restaurant. Two hours later, I was still visible, but not to my mother. She was nowhere. I tried calling her lobby, my lobby, her phone, my answering machine. I ran through every imaginable *Enquirer* headline. "Frail, elderly widow attacked in broad daylight." What had gone wrong? What had stopped her from making her way to the Chinese restaurant as she had countless times before? Eventually, I called her building again and heard from her doorman that she had been sighted in the lobby and was on her way upstairs. When I finally made contact with her and questioned her about her whereabouts, she was belligerent. There was a tone in her voice that I had not heard before. I knew that this was the beginning of a new time. Now when I looked behind myself, there would be no safety net. The hand I would hold would be my own.

My mother became a grand dame. Her auburn curls turned silver, and she didn't get around much anymore. A confounding dementia took hold and swept away everything but her spirit. She began to sing more than she talked—a lilting refrain of "Ooh la la." Maybe something she picked up in Paris. Eventually, even the singing stopped; everything stopped.

Now, a lifetime later, whenever I pass Riverside Drive, I feel both a comfort and uneasiness. It's been many decades since those evenings on the drive, and it has taken me this long to understand the unique balancing act between the pull of my history and the slow, steady motion propelling me forward. I frequently take the bus when I am there. When I emerge, I simply stand and watch. The cars are different. They are bigger, higher, bolder, but the colors are more somber. I try to count them, but they are moving much too fast.

The Doctor Will See You Now

It was a crisp fall morning when I, resolute and psyched for the cure, headed into my new periodontist's office. He had been highly recommended by my general dentist, and that was all I needed, for the choice was no longer my own; my gums had journeyed a greater distance from my teeth than was thought humanly possible.

"Hi" was the greeting from the perky receptionist as she slid past the celebrity memorabilia on the wall dividing those working from those waiting. After completing mountains of disclaimers, I was escorted to a cubicle with enough stainless steel to give "high tech" new meaning. I sat down, the chair reclined, and the periodontist appeared. A perfunctory greeting was delivered. My mouth opened on cue. No time was wasted; we got right down to basics: the X-ray. A barrage of numbers was bellowed as if I were at an auction. In no time at all, the periodontist was gone. In his place was a bevy of assistants busily conducting the "business" of my mouth, bickering noisily about the speed at which it was being done. I began to wonder—would things have been different had my photo graced the waiting room wall?

When the periodontist reappeared, I attempted to obtain the most basic information about my prescribed treatment and was briskly dismissed with the words, "That will all become clear at your next visit." Still attempting to clarify why I was there and what to expect,

I was reminded, as one would remind a recalcitrant child, "Now what happens at your next visit? We just went over that."

What's wrong with this picture? Are we as patients no longer being seen, merely being serviced—and poorly at that? When we are addressed hastily in restricted codes or with unnecessary circumspection, what happens to our feelings of comfort and confidence? All too often, we wait interminably in some small cubicle so our doctor does not have to wait, watching apparitions in white glide by without even a perfunctory acknowledgment until it is officially our turn. Certainly, this behavior does not promote healing. It is no secret that the inability of many physicians to speak intelligibly, using language understandable to a layperson, has negative consequences. Would any other service provider speak German if the recipient of the service only understood English? Various studies have actually shown that more than ninety million of us don't adequately understand basic health information when we leave a physician's office. This poor health literacy leads to increased emergency room visits, higher rates of hospitalization, and heightened medical costs. So why is a move to humanize health care only recently being put on the radar screen? Today there are actually programs joining art and medicine that train medical students to fine-tune their powers of artistic observation in the hope that those skills can then be transferred to patient care. More recently, several medical schools are implementing the multiple-mini-interview application process, which is the equivalent of speed dating for medical school applicants. This process requires candidates to analyze an ethical question with which they might be faced as doctors. An interviewer listens to the response within eight minutes. The candidates then move on to the next situation, providing rapid-fire answers. Only time will tell whether this is of any value, but the very fact that it is being incorporated into the process is significant and only underscores the need for more responsiveness and better communication among medical professionals.

I remember when my mother was hospitalized in a teaching facility and was expected to endure an onslaught of students descending on her room, ignoring any wish for privacy that she might have had. As she pulled her covers up around her neck, what would have been wrong with asking, "May we observe you today?" Every physician has the right to ask; every patient has the right to refuse.

We are talking about empathy here—about reading a person. That is the only road to true healing; there is no shortcut. And it is not about idle chit-chat, which serves only the doctor, not the patient. I have actually been to a gynecologist whose lips, while nestled between stirrups on which I placed my feet, kept moving incessantly, sputtering and chattering nonsense. Is that behavior more for the doctor's benefit or the patient's? We also do not need to know, while lying prostrate, about our doctors own personal medical nightmares. That is way too much information. Such disclosures do not build rapport; they are merely gratuitous, self-indulgent exercises that are better left out of the exam. There is only one sure-fire way to build rapport, and that is to listen and, yes, to empathize—to take a moment to pause, to reflect, and to ask the question, "What does this person really want to know?" And, of course, what kills rapport faster than the doc assuring us that all questions are welcome as he or she escorts us toward the door?

Just the other day, I had another experience to rival the one at the periodontist. As a result, my misgivings about the present state of health care and the proliferation of large-group medical practices have been confirmed. There was a time when a solo practitioner took the time to get to know a patient, particularly a new one. As a result of the relationship that evolved between them, that physician would be more acutely aware of the underlying medical issues that the patient might have. Examinations were not perfunctory exercises administered by anonymous assistants in large rail-station–like facilities. That style of practicing medicine simply does not work for me.

My most recent experience resulted from a call I had made to see a new physician, as I had been experiencing some disturbing symptoms.

First, there was an interminable wait in an overcrowded holding bin. Finally, after being ushered into a back examination room by one of the myriad assistants who were floating around, I underwent a preliminary exam. When the exam was complete, the doctor emerged and, without much personal interest, proceeded competently enough to perform several tests. There was limited conversation. Keep in mind, I had never met this person before. After administering an essential test, the doctor told me that I would need to return to the same behemoth of a waiting room where I had languished before. After an additional forty-five minutes, my name would be called to be retested so that a final diagnosis could be made. I was also informed before I returned to the waiting room that there was a possibility that the test I had just undergone might cause an uncomfortable reaction. Many reminders were given regarding the time at which my name would be called. But ultimately, when the designated time arrived, my name was not called. I was the one reminding the receptionist. At that point, I was once again brought to the bowels of the office to finish my exam, with yet another assistant. When I inquired about the final results, I was informed that the information would be given to the physician who had originally attended me. But it quickly became apparent that this physician had no intention of personally meeting with me again to discuss the test results. She only did so because she had been summoned by me and had little choice. Even worse, my husband had accompanied me this time, and upon seeing him, she extended her hand and formally introduced herself to him. At first, I felt a ray of hope. This was the first encouraging gesture I had seen that day. There was only one problem: he was already her patient!

This experience is an example of the shabby, no-frills health care that has become more and more prevalent today. Time constraints and too many patients make for bad medicine. No one should ever leave a physician's office feeling compromised and without answers. Dignity, mutuality, and respect must be restored to the physician/

patient experience. Much can be improved by a subtle mix of new behaviors. When the interpersonal is left out of a physical exam—when our health-care professional is adorned in a white coat and we are wrapped in paper—it is not a level playing field. When our doctor is addressed as "Doctor" and we are addressed by our first names, it is not a level playing field. And when nonverbal communication suggests a disconnect from what is being said, a large elephant moves into the room!

Unfortunately, much too often, patients are intimidated by physicians and simply react to what their doctors say instead of being proactive in securing the information and reassurance they may need. Concierge services guaranteeing unlimited access to physicians for a fee, often an exorbitant one, are springing up everywhere. But why should the payment of huge amounts of money, which many of us cannot afford, be necessary to have access to quality health care?

A recent *New York Times* article stated that the average physician today has two thousand patients. Now, we all like to feel needed, but maybe that is simply too many. So, how's this for an idea? How about scheduling one patient for one time slot and spending the time necessary to determine who they are instead of merely looking at how they are? Would that be so bad?

And also, just for starters—how about you, Doc, be Jane or John, and I be Roberta?

Does that sound like a plan?

The Conversation

We never managed to talk about his death; Bob was gone before we had the chance.

Had we gotten around to it, he probably would have sat in the corner of his worn, denim-striped sofa, the one he was looking to change when he got well, and told me dying was no big deal. It just got in the way of things.

Many times I sat across from that sofa with pretzels and a seltzer— or sometimes a scotch, but always with an eager ear. Bob was wise and seemed somehow strong and indestructible despite his health trials, of which there were many.

"You look good," I'd say, noticing the still-generous paunch that proudly declared itself beneath his burgundy turtleneck despite years of tests, treatments, pills and procedures.

"Hey pal," he'd bellow, "I'm getting tired of this. How long am I going to be the patient?"

Half knowing the answer, I'd feign a look of reassurance, maybe even speak a few words of comfort. But that night at home, I'd agonize— what if? I'd think the unthinkable and practice over and over how the good-bye would go, feeling almost as if I were rehearsing some morbid drama, knowing there was still a chance that I might not get the part. That was my hope.

Bob was a show biz kind of guy with a big personality and a Billy

Joel smile; I first met him at NBC, where we both had jobs. He was a senior radio executive; I was a program host. For most of my time there, we had only a passing acquaintance—one that passed as quickly as the canapés and wine at the press parties where we would see one another. It wasn't until the network no longer played a role in either of our lives that fate took a hand and placed us on the same midtown sidewalk enough times for us to begin meeting on purpose. That's how we became friends. The relationship continued for some twenty years, the last ten punctuated by the intermittent bursts of agony Bob suffered at the hands of his health.

I remember the good days—the hard-edged banter only true friends can manage, and also the sweetness. When my plaintive messages on his answering machine were recognized as such, I'd get an immediate call back. "Just checking in—you didn't sound right."

Our conversations were often the stuff dreams were made of. There were stories of radio and film stints, exotic trips, and blessings from children. And then there were the nightmares: the bypass surgery, the stroke, the prostate, the pacemaker, and finally, the cancer. I wondered when his resolve would give out.

"No change," he'd rejoice as his treatment progressed. I'd hear hearty acceptance of the consolation prize. First place—the big prize, the cure, was out of reach. He actually considered himself very lucky that his condition hadn't worsened and gave up on hoping that it might ever improve. But our conversations worsened, and our meetings became nonexistent. I'd call and hear a valiant attempt at bravado followed quickly by an urgent plea: "Gotta run."

I was scared but still held hope until that August day. As I followed the routine of a nondescript summer afternoon, Bob was rushed to the hospital for one last battle with his body. That day, he lost. In the space of a few hours, what was an ordinary Sunday in my life became a milestone in his. It seemed we should have shared it.

The urge to pick up the phone and dial that familiar number with the vibrant voice at the other end rocks my consciousness more than I could have imagined. Like an intoxicant for the addicted, friendship makes the moment go down easy. It numbs every painful jab and reminds us that it is once again possible to feel empowered, spirited, needed.

I want to know how it is for Bob now, but we never got to talk about his death. He was gone before we had the chance.

Lessons of a Christmas Cactus

What can be more fickle than December light? I didn't trust it that morning. The winter solstice was less than three weeks away. By that time, everyone in the Northeast had made a firm commitment to serious weather. The brittle, lacquered gray of dying branches only held life in the imagination.

As I began my ritual watering of the plants on my windowsill, I noticed a flat, vegetable-like cactus shouting for attention. Could it be? Almost Christmas, and something crimson was burning the tips of its outstretched arms, commanding me to celebrate the surprise. But the day was calling—so much for surprises.

I was on my way to my mother's. She had recently turned ninety-two. I had no time to waste. Five years ago, some confounding dementia had taken hold of her, turning our worlds topsy-turvy. Half-written checks, unpaid bills, and assorted credit card receipts lay peering out from under mounds of crumpled paper, defiantly challenging me to continue her unprecedented acts of neglect. I began attending to the never-ending details of a life not mine.

No thank-you note appeared. My mother seemed to regard her fierce independence as a God-given right. I was held in contempt. Dutifully, I forged ahead, with no choice but to see my emerging scars as a badge of courage. I kicked and screamed at the obligations, laughed at the saddest silliness, and cried at meager moments of triumph. I heard my name.

She knew me! Her confusion came in fits and starts and punctuated conversations with oblique references. What were the untold stories that a relationship of over half a century couldn't uncover?

We had been soul mates, after all—a team during my father's torturous decline and subsequent death from cancer some forty years before. Together, we had picked up the pieces and moved from a life of old-world grandeur in a cavernous apartment on Manhattan's Riverside Drive to the broad boulevards and leafy cul-de-sacs of Forest Hills, Queens. So why was this so hard? Wasn't there some way to retrieve the middle–of-the-night mother only a child could know?

"Get out, stinker," she would bark at anyone assisting with her daily care. "Stinker" never got much play in my household. That term of "endearment" was reserved for others who had not been blessed with my mother's consummate good taste. I wondered what she would have thought of her own behavior years ago. Carmen, her caregiver, assured me it was not personal. That was exactly the problem. Nothing was.

I watched Carmen, with her silky russet hair and large olive eyes that suggested a certainty about things. I remembered worrying when I first met her how she would do in a terry robe, clutching the bars around the bathtub. She was Spanish and had that well-healed look of someone who lingered in Madrid's late night hot spots till dawn.

"Have you ever worked with an Alzheimer's patient?" I asked. "They can be unpredictable and even insulting."

"My son Ritchie has Down's syndrome," she said. "I can handle anything."

That became clear on one of her first visits with my mother to the doctor. I braced myself for the ordeal of getting my mother from the wheelchair into the taxi. I watched, with amazement, how with the effortless moves of an Olympic gymnast, Carmen flipped my mother into the seat of the car as the warrior at the wheel waited impatiently.

"I haven't got all day," the driver shouted.

"You won't need it," she gently replied.

"Robertita," she called to me where I stood on the sidewalk, the color drained from my face. "We'll catch you later."

The car pulled away, tires screeching. The last image I saw was my mother's scowl at being forced into submission and Carmen's broad coral smile, eyes hiding behind formidable DKNY sunglasses. Her unwavering calm was mesmerizing.

Although I had irretrievably lost the parent I had known, a spirited, almost robust person had replaced her in the frame where I had begun to place an image of hopelessness. The hardness softened if only I looked. And so I found a way to look with new eyes when the funds to keep her at home started to diminish, when the government bureaucracy stood uncompromising, brandishing dates and demands that held for ransom the life we had known, when days seemed so dark and filled with the minutiae of her decline that only the sweetness of still having her got me through.

Whenever I came to visit, I'd have her wheelchair positioned parallel to where I sat so that I'd be able to hold her hand, stroke her hair, and breathe the gentle scent that had suffused my dreams of motherhood for as long as I could remember. She was the same. Only the language was different. I carefully chose my outfit whenever I saw her. She always noticed. Once, during the dizzying flushes of a fever, she even managed to whisper with smiling eyes, "I love my fancy girl."

With each condolence note I wrote to friends suffering the loss of their parents, I managed to find big rewards in small moments—a recognizable greeting, a familiar glance. It's not that I had ever marked our time together, but suddenly I cherished it.

I am continuing down a road that is bumpy and has few rest stops. There's no telling where the turnoff might be or when, and the fear that it will come before I am ready terrifies me. How can I be ready? But on a good day—and there are those—the sky is bright, the air is soft on my face, and there are things to look at along the way. I don't even notice the bumps.

I think of the Christmas cactus on my windowsill, and I smile.

Mother's Day

To My Daughter

May is here—the time for black caps and white dresses, the moment we waited for through winter's long siege. We didn't think we'd get through it, but we did. Storms were fierce, and golden light was hard to come by. Now it is abundant; the hot, sweet yellow ball burns almost too bright. We struggle to see.

Under a similar light, I held you once, tightly in my arms. Nothing stirred. Your smile thanked me for your treasured place in the world. That smile was enough then, more than enough. I kept a watchful eye—that's what mothers do. Motherhood was not something that came with a manual. Just when I thought I had nailed it, somehow I came up short. But there were moments sublime like the time we spent hours selecting the little school shoes.

"Yes- she has plenty of room to grow," the trusted salesman assured us. And we wasted no time before repairing to the local ice-cream hangout, new acquisitions in hand. That evening, in the shelter of your bedroom, walls covered in paper of pink and white clouds, I heard you say, "Mommy, you're the best mother in the world."

Days later, I waited for you. Like clockwork, you came off the school bus in those little shoes, laces stylishly curled, jumping onto the sidewalk, your crooked-toothed smile as big as the universe.

But it changed. The little shoes became Doc Martens, sleek suede

Pumas, and finally stiletto-heeled boots in which you walked briskly away. But it was as it should be. Sometimes when we unexpectedly met in the street and you were surrounded by your friends, we did that awkward mother-daughter dance. The baton had passed.

Then there were the years of raised voices—missed opportunities for us both to explain what we really meant. And finally the day came for you to leave. College was the new world and home the old country. After just one weekend in your new life, you called late one night.

"Maybe college isn't for me," you said. My heart sank, remembering my own tempest at your age- just at the portals of adulthood, but so very young. I was glad to be on the other end of the phone. The years flew. There were many tests, spring breaks, visits home, and lunches together at Upper East Side Manhattan haunts. I'd catch ladies lunching with their eyes glued to our table, looking at me. If looks could talk, they'd have been saying, "How did you get so lucky?"

What they didn't know was that you even asked me once or twice, "Mom, do you think people might think we are two girlfriends?"

Through all the days that followed after your college graduation, I never noticed what an observer of life you had become. You astutely knew that childhood was eluding you and you'd better have a plan. And so you decided on law school, just like your dad had years earlier. How we strategized to make the key fit into the magic door to open your future. You worked hard for your goal—essays, courses, study dates in Starbucks. And then the news: you had been accepted to a fine law school. I knew those little shoes would go places.

And so the journey began—the agony and the ecstasy of it all. Just a few days into law school, you called. "Maybe law school isn't for me," you said. But you endured it all, from a category-five hurricane in New Orleans with an unprecedented, history-making aftermath to that famous grading curve. I knew you had your wings.

Today I sit on my terrace thousands of miles from you, anticipating your big moment in just four days. You can't imagine the lump in my throat and the joy in my heart. All my outfits are neatly packed. Your card and gift are in place. I am ready indeed, but I am not prepared. Nothing can prepare me for the day when you will walk those splendid steps, bedecked in cap and gown, to receive your law degree. This is the stuff dreams are made of. This is Mother's Day, not some Hallmark version. But this is really your day, and you will be magnificent. Savor and enjoy every moment.

I will be watching.

LADY IN RED

Ever since I can remember, California has been on my mind. I am a kid from Manhattan, where winters are cold and summers steamy, and where priceless views from rooftops often consist of weathered water towers crusted with soot. New Yorkers are survivors, I always heard, and that includes a fair share of homeless urbanites laying claim to their slice of the apple. Although by the time I left New York in 2007, some of my homeless neighbors were gone from the streets, I remember watching with amazement the resilience, determination, and resolve of those remaining. Say what you will, there are certainly those who consciously choose to live life on their own terms under pretty tough conditions.

It made me wonder what drives our choices, assuming that we even have them. But that is pretty much where it ended. I was always able to move quickly apace with my own life without giving it too much thought. When I moved to Sausalito, California, the southernmost town in the much-coveted wonderland known as Marin County, I no longer felt winter's bite or summer's intensity. The landscape was certainly a change, but one thing struck a similar chord: a homeless woman. I named her the "lady in red." This time, though, I was not as able to move quickly apace with my own life.

I didn't see the "lady in red" every day, but I saw her often enough for her to take up residence in my thoughts. She didn't look the part, at least in the conventional sense, except for her wagon chock-full of newspapers, crumpled bags, and a quilted blanket. She was good to go—anywhere or nowhere. I was mesmerized whenever I saw her. It was clear that she had a past that was dramatically out of sync with her street style. She wore crimson—a matching ensemble that could have graced the racks of Saks or Neiman Marcus. She was striking in a well-worn, faded-fashion kind of way, but there was that wagon. Her cheeks were delicately tinted a soft pink; her eyes were a penetrating blue. She had an air of being taken care of at the same time she appeared neglected. She looked as if just yesterday, everything had been different.

When I didn't see her for a few days, I felt a kind of sinking feeling—the kind that happens when the phone rings with bad news. But she was a stranger and had no real meaning for me.

I inquired at the local grocery store and found out that her name was Ann. I asked the shopkeeper, whom I had seen supply her with fruit and other nourishment, about her life. The shopkeeper told me that Ann had lived another life at one time and had actively chosen this one. She was fine and did not want any help.

I'd see her set up camp behind the library. One day, I even saw what appeared to be an abandoned newspaper on a nearby bench. No one was in sight. There was no evidence of Ann's wagon. I slipped the paper under my arm and headed to a lunch place where I unfolded my new acquisition. As I began to settle in, I noticed through the corner of my eye that there were wheels rolling by the bench, and I caught a glimpse of Ann. *The newspaper,* I thought. *It is hers, and I have taken it.* I hurried over to her.

"Is this your paper?" I asked.

"Yes," she responded.

"I'm so sorry I took it—I didn't see anyone."

She smiled and simply muttered, "Thank you."

After that day, there was not a time when she did not acknowledge me as I passed by. One time, she even remarked that there was a storm coming. I found myself tempted to invite her in, but she seemed to have a plan and to discourage any idea that I might have just by her body language.

"They are sending me to a hotel," she said.

I did not know who "they" were, and I wondered if she did.

Had Ann had a home in the hills? Was there a career or a job that went bad? Or maybe a lover, a spouse, or children? Had this red outfit gone lunching in high places? I was obsessed with the question of how Ann had gotten from there to here. I did sometimes see her in a café nursing a coffee, having a sandwich, and even chatting with a passerby. I actually saw her once at the supermarket on the checkout line, looking almost indistinguishable from her neighbors. The next day, she was back on the street, wagon in tow. At the end of the day, I wanted to see her climb stairs to a small retreat somewhere, one that was safe and warm and uniquely hers—a place where she would heat a meal on the stove and remove her mask of mystery. But I knew in reality that darkness would fall hard on her life, a reminder of everything she had left behind.

And then the days flew by without sight of her. It had surely been a month or two since I'd seen her. I could not live without knowing. I stopped in to the library and hesitatingly asked, "Do you know the woman, the homeless woman who stays out back? Where has she gone? Is she all right?"

I was reassured by the librarian that Ann had been moved into a facility and that she was fine. She had gone willingly, I was told, and was doing well. That put a stop to it; I would not see her again. I wondered for a long time, though, why it mattered. I did not know her, after all. Or did I?

Aunt Miriam and Uncle Max

Long before there were three-star restaurants, there was Aunt Miriam and Uncle Max's.

Aunt Miriam was my father's eldest sister. She married late in life and was childless, except of course on days when I visited. Those were the times when all her maternal impulses converged, and the result was like hitting the jackpot for both of us. It was pure indulgence for me.

I must have been around five or six when these afternoon visits began. With the exception of my mother's mother, who died when I was twelve and after having been ill for some time, I never really experienced grandparents. Aunt Miriam and Uncle Max filled that void for me.

Aunt Miriam was a petite woman with tightly curled gray hair. She was dressed in full business attire no matter the occasion: nylon hose, jacket and skirt. When I was dropped off at her apartment, I'd hear the clicking of her serious black pumps on the hardwood floor as she approached the door. When I stood on my toes to kiss her, I'd feel the slight hint of a tickle from a burgeoning whisker on her chin. Miriam and Max's apartment was a nondescript arrangement of three rooms in a prewar building on the corner of Ninety-Sixth and West End Avenue in Manhattan. It was furnished with hand-me-down mahogany pieces, white doilies on tabletops, and a few pictures on the wall, the most prominent of which was a framed portrait of Franklin Delano Roosevelt hanging in the entryway. One knew immediately where Miriam and Max stood.

But the kitchen and adjoining dinette were the heart of the house. At any time of day, you could smell butter melting on the stove. Mesmerized, I watched Aunt Miriam sway gently from side to side as she scrambled eggs the likes of which I had never known before or since, accompanied by crispy home fries. Nothing surpassed these meals for me—except maybe the lemon chiffon graham-cracker-crusted pie that she concocted for my birthday. To this day, that is birthday cake to me.

These unique delicacies would be placed on fine dishes resting on a beige linen tablecloth. As I consumed them, I would gaze past the Wedgewood plates on the wall, out the window to the far reaches of Ninety-Sixth Street, confident that all I needed was right there in that dinette. Great disappointment filled me whenever these visits had to be canceled. I remember one time when Miriam called to say, "I won't be able to pick you up this week because I have to do spring cleaning."

I instantly responded with, "I will help you."

"Then it will be okay," she assured me.

Uncle Max was an average-height, bald-headed man with glasses and shiny wingtips who appeared docile and, if not happy, content. Unlike Miriam's two brothers, who were physicians, he was a button salesman on Seventh Avenue. But to Miriam, he was a high roller. I heard countless times about how they had met one summer in the mountains and how he had swept her off her feet. To me, it did not matter that fortune had not knocked at his door; he showered me with luxuries as if he had been a giant of industry. There was never a time when we went out strolling down Broadway that we didn't end up in some toy store where I was promised a little treasure—as long as it met with the approval of my parents. It always did. Somehow I don't think Max ever even asked them. If I didn't come home with a toy, he found a way to slip me a dollar or two.

I never thought too much about what life was like for Miriam and Max when I was not there. What child ever does? All I knew was that it felt very good to curl up in Max's lap while he either read or sang to me. "I have a toothache, a bellyache, a pimple on my nose," he would sing, and I would laugh uncontrollably. It seemed those times would never end, but they did.

One August afternoon as Max left work, while he was crossing the path of a Kinney rent-a-car shop, a car hastily pulled out and jammed on the gas instead of the brakes. Max nearly lost his life that day; he did lose his leg. The news was a one-two punch for me—perhaps the first realization in my young life that nothing stays the same and that life can change in an instant. Miriam and Max never quite recovered, although there was the semblance of life going on as before. Max was fitted for a prosthesis and continued to sport the same wingtip shoes. He was encouraged to seek restitution from Kinney but was too mild-mannered and intimidated to proceed. Those early years of adversity for him turned out to be a trial run for later hardship when Max developed throat cancer and was unable to speak. He wore a white cloth covering his throat and was only capable of making guttural sounds. Eventually, the seething frustration that was building inside him needed to find the voice he no longer had. One day after I was newly married, my husband, Jeff, received a call saying that Max had hit Miriam in the head with a telephone upon learning that she had misrepresented her age. He was taken to the hospital for observation, and Miriam was treated as well. No severe injuries resulted—physically, at least.

Miriam and Max returned home, each with a clean bill of health, but this period of calm did not last long for Max. Shortly after that incident, he fell on his way to the bathroom one night, and we received another call to remove him from the apartment. It was over. Miriam chose to go to a nursing home soon after that and lasted well into her nineties with no discernible illness. I visited her whenever I could.

To this day, I think: who were Miriam and Max? As young children, we know only relationship; we do not know people. And maybe that is the way it has to be. I was "little Bobs" and they were Aunt Miriam and Uncle Max. That was simply the deal, and it was quite enough.

When Ninety Becomes the New One Hundred

So here's the rub: everyone talks about readjusting chronological age to meet new lifestyles and health-care advances—the new thirties, forties, fifties, etc. Sounds great. And it works until, of course, we approach the far reaches—the eighties and nineties. What then?

Let me tell you a tale of two mothers: Sara, my mother, and Muriel, my mother-in-law. The stories are very close to my heart; the thoughts contained herein are just one person's opinion, not an across–the-board indictment of anything. I am convinced, though, that there is an ever-growing disconnect between young old and old old age. In our zealousness to hold back time, we allow ourselves to fall into an abyss of self-deception about what will happen when we are no longer able to stave off the monster at the door—old old age. By young old age I mean the seventies and early eighties; by old old age I mean the late eighties and nineties.

My mother was always clear about what she did not want. As far as aging went, tests, tubes, probes, and all extraordinary means and ordinary institutions were to be avoided. Years after she had been widowed in her fifties and was in great shape, she used fewer of her moderate resources on entertainment and daily indulgences in the hope that she would secure a future of relative comfort and dignity in her old age. When her small rental apartment was converted to a cooperative, she deferred to me. I eventually purchased it, thus securing it for the years ahead. The stabilized rent enabled her to age at home. For her, keeping her home was key. When the time came and she suffered bouts of dementia, private funds and ultimately government assistance were needed for home care. Thankfully, because she had planned well, she was able to achieve her goal. As a result of her choice, her surroundings changed relatively little. To her dying day, even as her health declined, the plethora of unnecessary medications and procedures used to anesthetize residents in nursing homes were nonexistent. My mother took no medication. She remained impeccably groomed, had her wishes and preferences respected, and actually experienced a strong connection and friendship with several of her home health aides. All this was manageable because there was only one patient to serve, and there were no mandates from managers to do one thing in all circumstances. But my mother did sacrifice the social activity of her young old years by being at home. The independent and assisted living institutions do provide resort-like facilities and built-in systems of peer interaction that are intoxicating for the young old. My mother's activities had to be planned; otherwise, her personal contact with contemporaries would be minimal or nonexistent. In my opinion, this was a small price to pay compared to my mother-in-law's story. My mother preordained the track she would follow by making sure that she did not give up her own home. She realized early on that personal home care in an assisted living facility, for any length of time, is prohibitively expensive, and she was not prepared to end up in a nursing home. My mother-in-law did not think it through that way. They had similar financial resources but very different end of life experiences.

When my mother- and father-in-law moved to Florida in their mid-sixties, their lime yellow, tropically accented condo appeared to be the home they would have forever. It fronted a golf course that my father-in-law called "the most 'beauty-full' vista in the world." Their lives were socially expansive with dinners at the clubhouse, cars, and vacations. They led an active lifestyle that appeared enviable. It seemed that the grim reaper of time would not be calling. But it happened one day, as it always does. It starts with a fall or two. Then comes a hospitalization along with ensuing complications. My father-in-law— who, despite multiple illnesses, including cancer, seemed to have the constitution of a bull—was down for the count. My mother-in-law remained indestructible in her Bermuda shorts, mules, and golf shirt. As my father-in-law's condition deteriorated and he ultimately passed away, my mother–in-law made plans to leave her home. For one thing, her vision had diminished to the point that she had been declared legally blind. And then there was also the prospect of unbearable loneliness. She never even considered getting health care in her own home, because she thought of herself as well enough to manage with minimal assistance and was attracted to the seductive, resort-like assisted living facilities dotting the Florida landscape. The question of what would happen after an independent or assisted living facility was no longer viable never crossed her mind. And so she gave up her own home, and that was the beginning of the end.

Many independent and assisted-living facilities are eye candy for the elderly. Some are converted hotels that offer cheerful pastel rooms and large, airy public dining spaces where meals are provided amid the clatter of conversation. They provide a false sense of forever in those years of suspended agelessness. The fantasy that life will always continue with morning aerobic swim classes and evening lectures is nourished until one day it is all over—triggered by some emergency, or several emergencies, that precipitates a family meeting and ultimately a move to a nursing facility. Home has been irretrievably lost at that point, and life often begins a downward tumble into tedium, neglect, and sometimes even despair. One's choices are no longer one's own. And unless it is possible to be taken in by a family member, one is at the mercy of a relentless bureaucracy and has completely lost control over one's preferences, personal needs, and independent decisions.

When my mother-in-law was moved into a nursing facility, she was elderly with severely impaired vision but was certainly lucid, upbeat, and free of serious medical conditions. Whenever she took ill at the nursing home, even with something as minor as flu symptoms, she was sent to a hospital as there were no medical services readily available. These visits were debilitating, to say the least. When she returned to the home, it always took some time to rebuild her strength and her positive frame of mind. Her feistiness and resistance to being manipulated by the staff eventually resulted in her being moved to a unit that had a higher staff-to-patient ratio and would make it easier for her to be "managed." However, no one considered the impact of placing her in an area in which most of the residents suffered from more advanced degrees of mental and physical impairment. When the family fought this decision, they were essentially told that it was nonnegotiable. My mother-in-law's decline accelerated quite quickly in her new environment. After the move, on any given day she could be found in that large, airy dining facility among drooping heads, drooling mouths, and broken spirits. Without any specific diagnosis, she was medicated to the max with drugs such as the anti-psychotic Risperdal. When the medication was questioned, her family was told that the doctor had ordered it. But the doctor was a roving troubadour dispensing such medication throughout many nursing homes. It was simply a way for limited staff to manage unlimited residents and keep them in an anesthetized state. Sadly, after a short stay in her new unit, my mother-in-law's decline became apparent, and her fighting spirit diminished. She began to fit right in. That's when ninety began to look like one hundred.

I am not saying that all nursing homes are bad, simply that the staff-to-resident ratio is such that it is impossible to maintain certain standards. And when that reality becomes clear, it is exceedingly difficult to revisit the idea of living in one's own home with attendant care. The home is gone. And in most cases, the costs of retrieving it at this point are too great, and the personal disruption of routine is another major deterrent. And so the die is cast.

Late-life and end-of-life decisions are very personal and should be an individual's choice. But they must be made early on in the life cycle and with full knowledge of the potential outcome. Once they are made, often there is no turning back. I believe Sara consciously made these choices. Sadly, Muriel did not.

Once Upon a Time

While it's hardly like reading the funnies, flipping to the obit page these days seems a reasonable accompaniment to coffee and toast. But why is it so compelling? I look at this page, as many of my friends do, and glance away at the same time, as one would while viewing a roadside crash. It is not just the families of my baby-boomer contemporaries but some of my contemporaries themselves who make that list. When a familiar name appears, I get pulled back to a time when the thought of anyone I knew showing up on those pages was unthinkable. The memoriam notices also get my attention.

Recently, I discovered the name of a junior high school friend's mother on those sacred pages. I instantly boarded that fast train back to long ago, when the woman was vibrant and indestructible and I was a pubescent bundle of anticipation, stuck somewhere between the delicacy of childhood and the untamed longing of adolescence. Greta, my friend Judy's mom, was brought front and center to my memory. She was foreign, mysterious, and beautiful to me, then and now. She appeared to have stepped off the screen of every art house movie theater. Judy and I were just beginning our journey as women of the world; we had much to learn from Greta.

In those days, Judy and I walked the streets of New York's Upper West Side outfitted with knee socks, pleated plaid skirts hiked up to our navels, and sacks stuffed with Twinkies, an afternoon delight concocted from ersatz chocolate and vanilla cream. It took very little then. These treats were our rewards for jobs well done at the end of each school day. But Friday lunches were the pièce de résistance. On those days, joined by Toni, another classmate, we would descend on Gitlitz, a Broadway delicatessen that played host to the entire population of the all-boys prep school, Collegiate, right down the street from our school. There we'd pool our resources and buy mountains of greasy fries. After raising the hormone level of each and every Holden Caulfield in the crowd, we would depart for the stoop of the coveted West End Avenue brownstone, which we aptly named the "dugout." We would then abruptly shed the good, nutritious bags of turkey, carrots, apples, and peanut butter that our mothers had packed and replace them with the soggy, oil-soaked sticks that were stashed in our book bags. It never occurred to us that the family that laid claim to the "dugout" had no idea that the place was also home to a trio of giggly thirteen-year-olds every Friday at noon.

It had been many years since I had been in touch with Judy, but I knew I had to write her a note. Of course the note would be for me in some small way, as I was mourning a time. Judy was of course, mourning her mother. I couldn't help but wonder. Had the years been good to Greta? Did she age like a Bergman heroine? Was she vibrant right to the end?

I sent the condolence note and waited. Judy and I lived on opposite coasts now. Although I probably would not see her, I knew where to reach her, as we had met serendipitously several years ago when I still lived in New York. While I recognized that Judy had much to contend with around her mother's death, I still would have been disappointed if I had not heard from her. Months passed until I saw her return address in the mail one day. How touched she was that I had written and that I remembered her mother. She said she would definitely call me if she ever came to California and that I should call her when I visited New York. She even made reference to my mother and the sweetness of the days we knew when we were young. She did call one day, and we met for lunch on one of my visits back East.

Is it just an elusive dream to take that fast train back? Is there a moment when opening that window on our past nourishes our present? And if we leave that window slightly ajar and peer through from time to time, maybe that isn't such a bad thing.

Cloud Nine

"I was on cloud nine once," she mused, the sweet strains of memory drifting by like the soft breeze on the promenade that day. It was the passing of a small pleasure craft along the river with the name "Cloud Nine" on its pastel frame that reminded Betty of the years of milk and honey.

When my mother first met her friend Betty, life was different. These warm, wonderful women were introduced by children and grandchildren at school pageants and park playgrounds. Although they lived only a few blocks apart, they were strangers until fate lent a hand. It seemed life's way of doing a good deed.

My mother had been alone for some thirty years. This was a world Betty had just entered; my mother knew the ropes. She managed Tiktiner, a high-fashion boutique at Bergdorf Goodman, for more time than I can remember. Just as effortlessly as she managed the boutique, she managed her life. She took great pride in her acknowledged ability to master almost anything, even the aching monotony and loneliness that can take hold over three decades of widowhood. When I even went so far as to suggest that she might consider retirement, she'd remind me that "Tik would never let me go." But she began to falter. Her fierce, unconditional independence gave way to cries for help. Betty, too, was losing her grip. She had been a school teacher and always seemed steady, resolute, surefooted, and strong. But suddenly she depended on a cane and no longer walked as if she had a purpose.

My mother and Betty walked gingerly toward unfamiliar territory. Both had been indestructible, with hairdos that were never neglected. Their days had always been chock-full of chores: banks, bakeries, and goodwill missions for friends were routine. They had known afternoons of tea and sympathy, chronicling life's big and small moments and comparing the ravages of time visited upon their cronies. But they had been rock solid. Now, it was their turn. Pilgrimages downtown were made infrequently and only to doctor's offices. Orthopedists' and ophthalmologists' numbers dotted the pages of their calendars. Pleasure was derived from sitting for hours by the river along the promenade across the street from their homes. With 172 years between them, they still had some time to kill.

Their children and grandchildren were in transition as well. The early awakenings of connectedness between my friend Gloria and me first took place in the hallway of my apartment, when we awkwardly spoke of matters unrelated to pediatricians and play dates. Since then, we have spoken of triumphs and defeats and have provided safe haven for each other during some dark days. Through Thanksgivings, Christmases, and more than one New Year's Eve, we provided a mutual support system that became our lifeline. Somehow, we also managed to have some fun. There were dinners en masse where sisterhood reigned! Across the generations, every style and age was represented. Our common bond was the determination to look life in the face and come out smiling. Yes, we had attitude—more than enough to go around.

I remember the Indian summer morning when I first saw my squeaky new kindergartner eyeing her classmate. Both wore crisply starched uniforms and moved with just a touch of skepticism toward an unknown destination. It didn't take long for a shy smile to turn into giggles and for a friendship to unfold. And then there were the sleepovers when no one got any sleep and the tribal necklaces that spoke volumes in two little beads: "Best friend." There were summers together in the Maine wilderness. On the threshold of full-blown adolescence, my daughter and her friend marched to another place—one where their mothers had been, or perhaps a different place. Three generations of women. The effects our families had on one another will not be realized for a long time, but what we do know is that the friendship was the music that kept us dancing.

My mother and her friend Betty still look for each other on the promenade along the river whenever the weather permits. They provide warmth during the late afternoon chill. They wear hats of canvas and straw and gloves to protect hands that have done the work of a lifetime. Exuberant, efficient helpers who "know best" wheel metal chairs to perfect spots in the shade. They speak animatedly of new recipes and old remedies—what ails and prevails. Their charges, my mother and Betty, eagerly await these meetings and look forward to some good, sensible conversation followed by bingo and a roast chicken dinner.

My friend and I still look out for one another whenever the other checks out for vacation. Mine was the face her mother saw in the emergency room when Gloria was off soaking up the Mexican sun. And hers was the face my daughter saw when a fracture at camp sent her to the hospital while I was touring the French countryside. Our daughters now buzz about dances, fashion—who's hot and who's not. And my mother and Betty still hang close. I am so glad that they have their gentle friendship. There is something so life-giving about it.

When I visit my mother and her friend Betty, I never stay too long. Who knows? Maybe they have secrets to tell or places to go where I have not yet been.

Cloud Nine—where is that, anyway?

PLACES

The real voyage of discovery consists not in seeking
new landscapes but in having new eyes.
—Marcel Proust

Ode to a Weekend House

It's Friday! The car is bulging with coolers, jackets, and CDs, and it's pointing north. The relentless din of the week is dissipating. Within the confines of the tan leather interior housing three eager travelers, only two sounds can be heard: that of the wind on the window and that of the DJ barking messages from the little box under the dashboard. Nestled inside are a trio of urban refugees seeking asylum in Connecticut.

This ritual is salvation for Manhattanites who have overdosed on city life. They flee to Connecticut, Long Island, and various other destinations in the hope of finding the antidote to what they've left. In these places, they are somewhere else. Even more important, they are someone else. Until this past August, my husband, my daughter, and I spent four years of weekends in a contemporary house in picture-perfect Sherman, Connecticut.

When we first caught the homeowner bug, we agonized over location. Rejecting the gentrified sameness of some of the towns on Long Island's East End, we opted for the easier commute and the Norman Rockwell–like feel of New England small town life. We stood in a local real estate office, oohing and aahing over capes, colonials, and contemporaries until one opened its doors. It was a formidable house to try out our country legs: five bedrooms, three decks, and a swimming pool. In no time, we realized we had made a huge mistake.

I remember the day we closed. In a nondescript white clapboard building set back from the road, amid signs offering dental, funeral, and optical services, we signed on the dotted line. Next thing I knew, I was roaming through the rooms of a vast foreign space like a settler in a new land. What history would be written there?

Our hopes were high, but the sheer size of the place was daunting. The rooms presented at least three more opportunities than we needed to experience water that wasn't hot, a population of uninvited rodents, and any number of structural details that had the potential to go awry. We were always calling an "expert" who would persistently need to be cajoled or coerced into showing up. As fast as something was fixed, something else was broken.

We never really had the chance to indulge our country fantasies. The wonderland outside our door suffered at the hands of seductive Route 7 outposts of domesticity—the answer to ex-urban ennui, Walmart and Home Depot. Saturday mornings were spent traveling along this route, packed as close as we were in the Lexington Avenue subway against cars strung like a necklace of multicolored beads waiting for the flashing arrow to lead us into temptation's way. I wondered how many other city renegades had left behind dreams of hiking, boating, fishing, or biking for a quick fix at one of these discount outlets.

And then there was December. It came with a vengeance. Did we really have to go this weekend? As we rolled along the highway where summer's leafy arbor had begun to resemble a prehistoric monster in its contorted winter dress, we were dreading the first blast of unwelcome air in our house. Layers of afghans took the place of heat; fleece and down were our friends. Pipes were frozen. We were dizzy with chores. Hearty locals soothed our wounded sensibilities far too often.

We hadn't gotten the message that, like the shrill fire alarms and the ubiquitous construction noise we left behind, these inconveniences went with the territory. It took almost all our time there to understand the delicate balance of country life and to accept its bounty. We put the place up for sale one year into the adventure. It took three more to sell. Every time we hit the Deegan on Sunday night, my husband would say, "It's not that I don't want a house. It's just that I don't want that house."

So back again to the tiny conference room with the gurgling water cooler. Someone had bought our house. How could she know what it was like to sink into the feathery lap of the giant club chair at dusk as the light played peek-a-boo through the double-height windows—or how it felt to spy on a newborn bird, its tiny torso rising rhythmically in its nest outside the door, or to watch the iridescence of dawn parting curtains of gold on Candlewood Lake. "There'll be another house," I would hear. So far, there hasn't been. We now collect local papers and have put out the word. We want a smaller house. We are veteran weekenders; all we need is another chance.

On my New York City terrace, I grow hibiscus plants and juniper trees. I am constantly enchanted by the cityscape outside my window. But no deer have made dinner out of my trees. No bird has made a home, and the thrashing water cut by jet skis on the lake is too far away to hear.

In Praise of Florida

It's easy to hate winter. But thanks to Florida, all that's changed. After spending countless winters in New York, the "center of the universe," off center is just fine. Down with down; I like spandex. There is just no substitute for an extra fifty degrees. On the days when the wind chill plummets, nothing on Broadway holds a candle to watching the weather channel in Florida. I have become addicted. As their weekly planner flashes across the screen, visuals of snowdrifts, plows, and weary plodders grab the attention. No, I have better things to do with my time, you say, but you just can't help but take a peek at the forecast promising sun and seventies.

For more decades than I care to mention, I've listened to the yuppie refrain—I hate Florida—while secretly lusting for just one sultry fling before throwing another log on. It's just not cool to like Florida. But let me tell you the best-kept secret: people are not going there to die—they are going there to live! I know. I did it too. I didn't choose one of the gilded enclaves along the coast. No, I went for the fringes of the big town: Miami. I took a semester off from my teaching job and arrived in early January in Key Biscayne, where I rented an apartment for three months. Key Biscayne is Florida's northernmost key, just off the south end of Miami. The colorful sign at the entrance to the Rickenbacker Causeway reads "island paradise." This stretch of road suspended over the unabashed aqua of Biscayne Bay follows a path of skyline and marinas carving a boundary between what lies behind and what lies ahead. The causeway separates miles of lush tropical land from the more beaten paths of the city. The actual village of Key Biscayne has its own seat of government, police, and firefighters and even its own cable TV channel. It boasts a golf and tennis facility, hiking paths, and an endless expanse of ocean. Condos line the boulevard; they are tasteful and welcoming. Gracious Mediterranean villas encircle the other side of the island. There are plenty of amenities—shops, restaurants, and a large recreational lawn referred to as the "village green." It is possible to walk everywhere around the island, no small feat nowadays!

No early birds! The majority of islanders are between the ages of twenty-five and fifty-four. The predictable homogeneity of South Florida imagined by many northern urban dwellers is not in evidence. Fifty percent of residents were born outside of the United States. Spanish shares the spotlight with English. In five weeks, I heard one siren and saw no evidence of garbage other than the giant collection tank rolling in to suck up waste.

Yes, there is life beyond the key. There is Coconut Grove, with its tourist-tapping open-air mall, Cocowalk. Its numerous shops, restaurants, and marinas are a mere fifteen minutes away. Vizcaya, the enchanting Italian Renaissance–style palazzo and garden, is nearby. Not far away is Fairchild Gardens, a vast botanical spread seductive enough to woo me back for several visits, where I substituted the obligatory arctic walk for coffee and the paper back home for several languorous hours under a fan of palms. But this all sounds very quiet. How does a purebred New Yorker get some action? Look around! South Beach rocks. Although the trendy sideshow has moved elsewhere and you are unlikely to see a tattoo passing for a bathing suit, the cacophony of sounds still roars louder than the ocean. Every designer shop imaginable has taken up residence, and on other areas of Miami Beach and throughout Miami, there is an ever-growing art scene—galleries, museums, a dazzling new concert complex in the works, and who knows what else. Certainly there is not a lack of something to do. That is, if you care to get out of your lawn chair.

So next time you want to curl up by the heater with a good book on a bad day, remember: in South Florida there are also good books, and there are almost no bad days. And oh, have I mentioned that the sun sets later? At nearly six in the evening, bathed in soft yellow light, I watched a gathering of birds congregating on a sand bar over the Atlantic. And then there's the moon. Have you seen the moon smiling down on a clear, star-studded night?

It's winter—come on down.

The Last Time I Saw Paris

It has been wisely stated that one cannot step into the same river twice. That is because the water that flows through it is always changing. Yet there is often the perception that what appears one way will forever endure in its original form and remain as if we were seeing it for the first time. But like that river, life flows in its own rhythm, and by the time the water reaches its bank, what is happening on shore may be a world away. And so we see with new eyes.

Paris exploded for me when I saw it for the first time on my honeymoon, when I was twenty-two. Actually, Jeff and I had not initially included it in our itinerary. We decided at the last minute to spend twenty-four hours there. Rain poured that day, but we managed to take it all in anyway—every beret-bedecked street artist, mime, and chanteuse, every alleyway and boulevard. We heard accordion sounds coming from rooftop garrets; even the abundant horse meat in cheap tourist bistros tasted like steak. For many years to come, any doughy, tasteless crescent roll passed for a croissant; street horns back home started to sound like the cacophony of Parisian traffic noise.

Through my United Artist film publicist years, in my early twenties, I had the good fortune of being hosted by foreign correspondents whenever I traveled. I benefited from their ample appetites for good food, good drink, and good expense accounts. Many kindnesses were bestowed in the name of publicity and burgeoning friendship. But friendship was a loose word in those days—it was simply a product of youth, fueling the very basic fires of laughter and fine fellowship. It wasn't even necessary to speak the same language. Smiles saved the day. Some of these connections lasted through the years and were effortlessly resurrected each time I found myself on foreign shores.

In the early days, Jeff and I became acquainted with two expats called Francoise and Franco. They were journalists living the dream in Paris. She was from Switzerland; he was from Italy. We'd make our way to their small apartment by going through a flowered courtyard and up steep flights of stairs to two small rooms lined with rows of books, muted carpets, and windows framed with wrought-iron curlicues. There was never a time when we did not receive a hero's welcome. The apartments changed every few years. Whenever an apartment was no longer affordable on a journalist's salary, they would move. We would be informed of their new digs, enter the contact information in our address book, and head to the next place for our visit. We were somehow never able to reciprocate their hospitality, except once at a rented summer house in New Jersey. But in Paris, Francoise and Franco were in charge. Dinners were enjoyed in small backstreet cafés with vases of abundant gladiolas in the window and proprietors acknowledging our hosts personally in their typical sing-song way: "Bonjour, Messieurs Dames," followed by mention of their names and inquiries into their well-being. This greeting delighted our hosts and stripped us of dreaded tourist status. It worked for everyone! Extravagant meals were consumed, and champagne flowed. Francoise was fluent in English; Franco was not. He struggled to communicate, and we struggled back. But we all managed. Curiously, it wasn't until years later, when Franco's English was much improved, that we experienced some awkwardness. At that time, it somehow became more important to speak the same language.

Our activities with them were carefully orchestrated and left little room for spontaneity. We saw them often when we were in Paris; they ran us ragged. But as time passed, their apartments became more temporary and were unavailable for guests. Eventually, these places morphed by necessity into "charming" Left Bank hotels they would find for us. It had become increasingly clear that journalism jobs were precarious and mere survival in the city they loved was a challenge. They were endlessly apologetic for what they perceived to be lapses in graciousness.

Last spring, Jeff and I returned to Paris after a decade away. It poured again, but this time it felt cold and off-putting. Several of the museums were closed due to a strike, the melodious-sounding horns on the street were shrill, and the accordion music coming from the garret was replaced by the persistent howling of the wind. It wasn't quite the mistral, but it sure felt like it. Small boutiques had become large designer emporiums or nondescript chain stores. A big sign was posted in our overpriced hotel stating that the computer was available for guests. It seemed, however, that the front desk receptionist had been firmly planted in the chair; she was facing the screen, typing furiously away, whenever I approached that spot. Merely asking when the equipment might be available for hotel guests, as suggested on the sign in the lobby, I received a chilly officious response: "Madame, I am working."

And last of all, our friends no longer lived in Paris. They had fled to Switzerland because the rents were just too high and they could not do it anymore. They did return to entertain us, but there was somehow a forced joviality to the evenings. They tried valiantly to keep it all going, but their absence from the place that meant everything to them weighed heavily on their spirits. They would still not permit us to reciprocate. It was painful to watch. The restaurants were more lavish, but our great good time was not.

Had Paris changed, or had we? We realized that we had left for all our other visits from New York; by comparison, Paris was mellow and charming. This time, we had come from California, where we now live; perhaps that made a difference. Francoise and Franco were trying their hardest to find a way back to Paris; meanwhile, there were heartfelt invitations to their new home in Switzerland and noises made about coming to visit us.

On our last day in Paris, we saw a young American couple walking arm in arm. They kept looking up at everything, just as we had years before, and appeared to be on their way somewhere—perhaps a place where they had not yet been. Once again, it was raining, but that didn't seem to change the unmistakable exuberance they had about them. For us, the city seemed different that morning. We wondered whether we'd be back.

Auf Wiedersehen, Yorkville: See You Now and Again

Among some of my fondest New York memories is the rich culinary patchwork of its restaurants. When I was a young child, on my birthday, my parents would take me to Chardas and Grinzing, two Upper East Side Hungarian restaurants with strolling violinists and accordion players. It was not just the succulent goulash and spaetzle that got me but the haunting gypsy music as well. I never forgot it. There were many such places in New York's Yorkville back then. Sadly, almost all of them are gone.

Yorkville is an Upper East Side neighborhood whose heart is Eighty-Sixth Street. Years ago, Eighty-Sixth Street was called "German Broadway." Lining the sidewalk were Biergarten-style restaurants, butcher shops with salamis and sausages dangling in the windows, and pastry cafés where many old-country afternoons were spent over strudel or maybe a schwarzwalder kirschtorte, a rich chocolate confection with an indecent raspberry filling oozing from all sides. Kleine Konditerei, Café Geiger, The Viennese Lantern, and Heidelberg, which still exists, are some of the most memorable. These places were old-world outposts in the new world where it was possible to consume overly large portions of hearty fare along with a heavy dose of nostalgia. There are now fewer and fewer of them.

But for me, there was nothing quite like Kleine Konditerei. I enjoyed many dinners with my mom there before she became too elderly and infirm to go out. I remember watching her walk down the block after we'd finished dinner, satiated and with a spring in her step, unlike what I had seen on the way in. Occasionally, I would meet friends there, or my husband Jeff would indulge me and take me there for my favorite: schnitzel holstein. Though it never was his favorite, Jeff wouldn't mind a decent sauerbraten every now and then. But that veal cutlet was unrivaled. It arrived at the table doused in bread crumbs, glistening and golden, flat like a pancake, garnished with anchovies and capers, and crowned with a sublimely runny egg. Alongside it were crusty, crunchy home fries, creamed spinach, and miles of red cabbage—pure ecstasy!

Yorkville, during most of the nineteenth and twentieth centuries, was home to Czechs, Germans, Hungarians, the Irish, the Jewish, the Lebanese, and the Polish. Many German residents migrated uptown from the Lower East Side. The numerous watering holes where people would gather for a hearty meal, a brew, or some pastry were like large communal living rooms or salons—the social pulse of a time and place. I miss having these gems at my doorstep. There is still Heidelberg restaurant on Second Avenue, the only remaining vestige of this genre in the East Eighties, with the same feel and the same winning schnitzel. But I live in Sausalito, California, just outside of San Francisco, now. Aren't there any German restaurants there, you ask? Of course, but I have not found one to equal my Yorkville experience. Maybe it's just the sweetness of youth and the memories of good times that can never be quite matched.

Whenever I visit New York, though, after much coaxing and cajoling, I talk Jeff into accompanying me to Heidelberg. He kicks and screams, but let's face it: at Heidelberg, even the wursts are the best. Jeff, too, looks happy on his way out the door.

High-calorie meals like these German ones are certainly no longer in vogue. Plates decorated with minimalist vegetables and splattered color are more the rage. Vast white space on the plate commands serious money at trendy restaurants these days. But for me, there is still something to be said for this industrial-strength food and the kitschy, homespun flavor of these places. They are a treat every so often. Even the waitstaff look merry in their lederhosen. It's almost like an evening away for the price of a meal. And after a few Dinkelakers, emerging out the door onto hardcore urban Second Avenue is just enough of a jolt of reality to keep me wanting to come back.

EAST MEETS WEST

We must be willing to get rid of the life we've planned,
so as to have the life that is waiting for us.
—Joseph Campbell

A Touch of Zen for the World Weary

In New York, my husband Jeff and I planned the ultimate escape. I was committed to a two-week teaching stint on the Berkeley campus, and then we would take off. Heading south from San Francisco, we'd meander through hillsides nestled in the Santa Cruz mountains, make a brief stop to check out Point Lobos, and then wend our way further down the Monterey peninsula for the pièce de résistance: a few days drooling over the otherworldly wonder of Big Sur's Pfeiffer Beach. We had some time open, though, and maybe—just maybe—although it was last-minute, the Tassajara Mountain Zen Center would have room. We'd come upon the place in a hidden California guidebook, and it seemed just the antidote to the stresses of big city life. We called from New York only to find that they were booked solid and had been for months.

"We could put you on the waiting list," the gentle voice on the phone suggested. As soon as we agreed, we forged ahead with our plans, not trusting the remote possibility that this adventure would ever come to pass—until we hit Big Sur with still a day to fill. My husband pulled a tiny slip of paper out of his pocket with "Zen" scribbled on it. It was worth one more try. The same gentle voice told us that there had been a cancellation but he would have to call those on the waiting list first. While we held in Big Sur, he called us in New York. Was it karma or just good luck? We were starting to feel more spiritual! We received the go-ahead and detailed driving directions. We began to get excited. But we were hardly prepared for the grueling fourteen miles up and down a steep, unforgiving dirt and gravel road. The road snaked around cavernous rocks and didn't appear to be wide enough for our car, let alone another car coming in the opposite direction. Fortunately, we never saw one.

Tucked in the trees amid the Santa Lucia mountains and the Ventana wilderness outside Big Sur, at the end of a dust-sprinkled parking lot, a sign reads "Tassajara Mountain Zen Center." Lining the perimeter of the lot are several wheelbarrows used to transport luggage onto the grounds. Not that anyone needs much. No bellman awaits you, no welcome cocktail, no pop of a distant tennis ball, only the gurgling of the nearby creek and the hushed voices of visitors hearty enough to make the trip. The landscape is simple. Leafy trees form a canopy over unpaved walkways. The scenery is not dramatic, but it is somehow life-giving. Tassajara is a working Zen monastery. It is only from May until October that guests are welcome. During that time, the resident monks and students have a mission to serve visitors and to maintain a strong connection among hosts and guests.

It was late when we arrived. After being shown to our room in the stone house (there are also redwood cabins, yurts, and dorms), we received a briefing on the Tassajara way of life. We were told how to use our lanterns, which would be the only form of light in our room. We were told about the hot plunge tubs in the bathhouses, which were single-sex until the evening, when the monks held meditation. At that time, they became co-ed, with clothing optional. There were no showers in the rooms, although some rooms had sinks and toilets. All showers were communal. My husband and I headed for the zendo, a formidable structure where zazen evening meditation was held. We obediently removed our shoes before entering. We were eventually directed to various cushions facing the wall. The stillness was astonishing. Never before had silence made so much noise.

No one budged until several gongs were heard and ritualized bowing and chanting began, followed by an orderly exit. At that point, we were so relaxed that my husband grabbed the wrong sandals among those lined up on the deck outside. A restful night followed. The morning was ushered in with a full breakfast served in a rustic communal dining space. Guests gathered in a courtyard, where they retrieved their linen napkins from the previous meal and joined other guests for a veritable feast. The food was vegetarian and plentiful. Carnivores were converted daily through masterful artistry in the kitchen. Meals consisted of lush concoctions of berries, grains, greens, tofu, and more. Liquor wasn't served, but it was not frowned upon. Some guests brought their own wine, and caffeine was available. Meal practice was taken seriously. After breakfast, activities were limited, but no one seemed to miss the programmed recreation of conventional resorts. There was a swimming pool refreshingly devoid of restless, hyperactive revelers screaming "Marco Polo." Guests were respectful of an unspoken noise code. Children were not unwelcome, but their presence was not encouraged either. The brochure suggested that it might be a good idea to experience Tassajara alone before bringing children. "Serene" is the operative word.

The center is one of three in the area; the other two, the San Francisco Zen Center and Green Gulch Farm, are located in San Francisco and Marin County, a short distance from the city. Tassajara is modeled after Zen mountain retreats in China. Shunryu Suzuki, a direct spiritual descendant of the great thirteenth-century Zen master Dogen, founded the centers. It is said in his book *Zen Mind Beginner's Mind* that "In the beginner's mind there are many possibilities but in the expert's mind there are few."

The beginners I met at the center were easily seduced. Willingly, these guests shed their reliance on common creature comforts like hot water in their rooms, electricity, telephones, television, and radios. Fax machines and cell phones seemed to be nonexistent. For those who needed to be outfitted with a laptop, there was an hourly electricity fee for recharging. The limitations didn't seem to bother anyone—on the contrary, they were part of the experience. Even after one day, we felt a mind/body alignment and revitalization unlike any we had experienced in holistic resorts or wellness spas. The goal was not to "do" anything different, rather simply to "be"—to listen, to accept, and ultimately to follow a basic Buddhist principle: finding perfect existence through imperfect existence. In Shunryu Suzuki's own words, "if you had a limitless life it would be a real problem for you." At Tassajara, it is not the absence of contemporary life's trappings that is the problem; it is returning to them.

EASTERN BLOCK

I left home this year—home as in the Big Apple. New York had been action central for me for longer than I care to remember.

"Be careful of what you wish for." Well, I was careful—very careful. I thought long and hard, and after much deliberation and two three-month tryouts, my husband and I took off for what is often called "the left coast"—California, some three thousand miles from the friends, jobs, dentists, and restaurants we held dear. We wanted a different life—mountains instead of skyscrapers. We chose Sausalito, a poor man's Mediterranean hill town some seven miles across the bay from San Francisco. Don't get me wrong. Poor has nothing to do with cost of living or demographic—quite the contrary. It only suggests that the ubiquitous fantasy of escaping to a land of orange trees and cafés can be possible while still speaking in your native tongue. There are colorful hillside houses, restaurants along the water, fishing boats in the harbor, and even an ochre-crusted fountain downtown in the main square.

When we arrived, it was summer. But summer doesn't hold the same magic in Northern California. It can be foggy and damp, for one thing. Even if it is sunny and warm, which it was our first summer, not nearly as much rests on the season. "Back East," as we now say, those few months called "summer" are the big payoff, and they are fleeting. The knowledge that all that lush indulgence will end so soon ups the ante. Here, vibrant flowers can be had all the time, for a price. Not that there aren't seasons, but the changes are far subtler, and much of the sensuousness of summer can linger even in chilly temperatures. A Meyer lemon tree thrives on my patio in January. There is a deal made here: you put up with nature's wrath—mudslides, earthquakes—and you get nature's bounty. It can be a land of harsh awakenings, but somehow balance is always restored. Sunrise moves quickly from red to gold. Perhaps that is why it is called the Golden State.

Easterners tend to have a love/hate relationship with the West Coast, particularly New Yorkers. There is the thinking that all this good cannot be good for you; that soul building lies in suffering and in knowing that darkness cannot predictably be relieved by light. But let me tell you, it can. And too much of a good thing can be very good! That is the dirty little secret. In fact, light, when radiating deeply, has a way of making us feel more joyful, maybe even more peaceful, and less tough to the core.

One balmy fall day, early on, I was lunching outdoors with a friend at a sidewalk café. Nothing seemed to spoil the bliss. Oh wait—there was one small thing, and not so small at that! A big truck with its motor idling was parked right across from the restaurant. It did not smell or sound very good. The driver sat at the helm totally oblivious to the power he had to ruin nirvana. I started to plot my attack. I rose gently from my chair, careful to conceal an arrogant certainty that I already knew the outcome of the request that I was about to make. I was planning to use my best California-ese to ask—to plead—"Excuse me, would you mind turning off your motor?"

But I never got the chance. He saw me approach, and with an extravagant, all-knowing grin, he deftly turned the ignition to the off position. I smiled. He smiled. I returned to my seat. Minutes later, he pulled away from the curb. I mouthed the words "thank you." He returned them with, "you're welcome."

Now, we can argue that this was just one sweet, beefy guy, not a whole state's worth, but I contend that this was one sweet, beefy

California guy. Not that there isn't a generosity of spirit in New York or anywhere else in the East, but—correct me if I'm wrong—in New York, truck drivers don't graciously accommodate the needs of diners. There are simply too many truck drivers and too many diners. It's just the way it is.

But sometimes this out-and-out friendliness can be over the top! I remember ducking out the back door of a hotel I was staying at in California because the persistent well-meaning chitchat from staff at the front desk was just too much! Bad moods seem to manifest differently here. It must be one of the rules of the place—and places do have rules. Before I came here, I must admit I was a member of the club. I often subscribed to the thinking that this place was nice to visit—but how could anyone possibly take it as a steady diet? Curiously now, many of the Californians I meet are transplanted Easterners and, in some cases, New Yorkers.

After an energetic walk on a fragrant, pine-scented path climbing to a mauve, misty gray summit or a walk on a rocky beach minutes from home on an ordinary Sunday, life can look so good that an earthquake seems more manageable than a snowstorm. By the way, there is snow here in this part of California but you have the option to go to it; it doesn't come to you.

So how about Madison Avenue, Greenwich Village, a concert in Central Park, or some of the staccato rhythms of the boroughs? Do I miss them? You bet I do, but not because they offer more. It is not a question of more; the two are just different. New York, after all, is my story, and stories have a way of taking on lives of their own.

I am returning to New York for a visit soon. Maybe when I am warmly wrapped in layers, in my car on the Long Island Expressway on a February afternoon, I will hear the strains of "California dreamin' on such a winter's day."

New York, New York

As our plane descended on Manhattan's charcoal canyon of dreams, gliding past rows of neatly ordered suburban sprawl, my husband and I watched—all eyes fixed on the prize.

In the distance were the monoliths of desire we knew all too well. At once there was a dizzying drop into heart-stopping wonder; the dazzling behemoth called New York was spread before us.

Being a native, I never experienced New York for the first time. It was simply there, and so was I. It is only since I have left that it has come truly into focus. The thrill of the place is undeniable, but just as an old fighter who repeatedly enters the ring eventually wears out, each encounter takes its toll. After a few days, I was beginning to wear out.

But on this last June afternoon of my visit, the planets were in perfect alignment; the sun sparkled, and Central Park beckoned like a lost lover. We rode the carousel that day and later welcomed dusk with a crimson Campari at The Boathouse restaurant overlooking the lake. In a Third Avenue pub, we feasted on thick, juicy burgers decadent enough to be illicit. It was intoxicating, and the familiarity of it was seductive. Later we slept peacefully but awoke to the roar of horns blasting along the avenue. The next morning, satiated and serene, we boarded another plane that would take us across this great land over the Sierra and ultimately to a place we now call home—California.

Nature and Nurture

More than a quarter of a century ago in Ulster County New York's Shawangunk mountains, I caught the bug: a lifelong outdoor habit that is with me to this day. Oh, I'd had touches of it before—mild outbreaks in Riverside and Central Parks, on Long Island beaches, and while summering on the Cape—but nothing with as much strength and persistence. I knew then that I would chase every opportunity to venture outside—a challenge for a kid growing up in the most urban of cities, New York.

On the Hudson River's west side, just past the south end of the Catskills, is Lake Mohonk and its jewel of a Victorian castle, Lake Mohonk Mountain House. Designated as a national historic landmark, the resort was built sometime between 1879 and 1910. The property, reminiscent of Europe's grand palace hotels, has attracted famous guests from Howard Taft to Theodore Roosevelt and Thomas Mann, but the seduction for me was the nearly seven thousand adjoining acres of the Mohonk preserve, a network of wooded paths, rocky outcroppings, and, of course, the clear glacial lake that spans half a mile of the landscape. Just setting foot there was magical. On the drive up, I was like a child anticipating an amusement ride. When I left, I just kept wanting to go back. I brought all my friends. There was a clear filtering of the week left behind once I donned my hiking boots and grabbed my walking stick.

What was the draw? It is the same reason armies of vacationers descend on our national parks each year. Wallace Stegner suggests in *Crossing into Eden* that we visit such places as the American wilderness for our "soul's good." Modern thinkers postulate that such exposure may even contribute to our "mind's good." A University of Michigan study demonstrated that people actually learn more effectively after walking in the woods than they do after similar activity on a busy street. I believe the air simply feels better, and all that weighs heavily seems manageable. There is an undeniable clarity and sense of well-being. Spending time outdoors heightens our recognition that there is still much we do not know about this mysterious universe and that all creatures have a part in it.

Now ensconced thousands of miles from Lake Mohonk, I find my setting on a hillside in Northern California a feast for any nature enthusiast. Just walking in the Marin headlands, which are practically outside my door, is an adventure. On a Saturday afternoon in summer in Point Reyes National Seashore, if I happen to cross the path of a herd of Tule elk, I consider myself lucky. Tule elk herds had virtually disappeared from California in the late 1800s only to be reintroduced over a century later. And now at Tomales Point, on the outskirts of Point Reyes National Seashore, over four hundred of these graceful creatures roam, making the area home to one of the largest populations in the state. If I am fortunate enough to see them, I will, of course, only observe them from a distance; proximity might make them nervous. The best way to view these animals is through spotting scopes or binoculars. Their antlers punctuate the Western sky with a stark geometric beauty. No, this is not some Ralph Lauren setting. This is the real deal! Every weekend during summer, park volunteers and tourists gather for a peek at these elk. But through the rest of the year, there are also opportunities to view elephant seals, whales, and birds. On any given weekend, on a winding path, dotted with fuchsia and orange wildflowers, particularly in early summer, I push back the breeze as I walk briskly, descending toward the sea, and toward an immense pristine stretch of beach called Mc Clure's at the tip of Point Reyes. I am extravagantly rewarded for my modest exercising of muscles. All at once, a fusion of yellow light curls around the never ending blue of water and sky as they meet. I feel privileged, as if I've gained entry into some elite club, but of course, all of this is free for the taker. It is a dazzling party yielding abundant joy.

Wilderness fine tunes our attention; it makes our focus effortless, makes possibilities seem vast. It renders our senses as uncluttered and pure as if we were seeing everything for the first time, just as I did that day when I was eighteen at Lake Mohonk.

A Place of the Heart

Just as the early-morning light filters through my window, I rise to finish loading my car.

I take inventory: jackets, fleeces, sun protection, hiking boots, and Tchaikovsky's Fifth Symphony, which will be my valued companion, along with my husband Jeff, for a good part of the journey along California's Highway 1—destination Big Sur. The trip to Big Sur from my home in the San Francisco Bay Area takes just under three hours. As we glide down the road, a sense of anticipation takes hold. Nearly two hours out, I see signs for the Monterey peninsula, and that's when it begins: pure exhilaration.

As we work our way down, the road starts to curve and begin its embrace with the Pacific. When we approach the northern part of the Big Sur coast, there sits the historic Bixby bridge with its 320-foot arch, welcoming me home. I flood the car with my music, and now I am gone—totally gone. I see other travelers pulling off the road to gawk at the majesty outside their window, but I am way beyond that. I continue to ride past the marbled cliffs and rainbow-tinted hills. I watch the redwoods and Monterey cypresses as they stand firm in the breeze. The landscape is grand and self-assured; one gets the feeling that it knows exactly its effect. The very breadth of its heartbreaking beauty is enough to shake the everyday out of anyone.

The early Spanish settlers gave Big Sur its name—the big country to the south. And it is big indeed, both in size and in spirit. The overall area covers about 192,000 acres, and I want to explore every inch. Just the persistent motion of the crystal foam dancing with the waves of the ocean in an endless tease is mesmerizing. In this setting, at this moment, there is nothing standing between me and pure bliss. The music in my car is moving toward its conclusion. Other than the last strains of the orchestra, there is no sound. I look at Jeff, and we both know that there is no place on earth I would rather be.

The sheer expansiveness of Big Sur is affirming. Even when a stream of smoky, unrelenting fog obscures an otherwise perfect summer afternoon, I forgive. Just as the California condors, with their amazing wingspan, float overhead effortlessly, joy envelops me with ease. All at once, the great secret is out: in this land of so much, we need so little. There is no town of Big Sur, no sidewalks to stroll, no locking arms toting shopping bags, no latte stops or cineplexes, just a succession of rustic lodges, a post office, a grammar school, a health facility, and a few modest eateries. And, yes, the two hedonistic palaces. The Post Ranch Inn and Ventana Inn are just down the road, and rooms can be had for a small fortune! They are tasteful and blend sublimely with the environment, but in a place where the stark natural backdrop is everything, the price for anything more is dear.

Perhaps the attraction of Big Sur is that it seems to be what we all seek—pleasure and peace. It is a place where a walk on a beach with massive rock formations creating umbrellas over the sand or time spent gazing at a waterfall cascading down a sheltered cove is all the entertainment we need. There are other coastal environments of great beauty, but they are somehow not Big Sur. I sometimes think that the environment of Big Sur is so much larger than life that it does something to our inner landscape. The writer Henry Miller, a one time resident, said it best: "Paradise or no paradise, I have the very definite impression that the people of this vicinity are striving to live up to the grandeur and nobility which is such an integral part of the setting." He also noted that "there being nothing to improve on in the surroundings the tendency is to set about improving oneself."

Some of nature's greatest forces comprise what we call Big Sur; the menu of offerings is extensive. There are myriad trails, abundant wildlife in the Ventana wilderness, parks for camping and picnicking, and just about every primitive vista you can imagine. The land is divided into three regions: the North Coast, Big Sur Valley, and the South Coast. The stunning visual feast that abounds provides a rich resource for the true outdoor enthusiast or even just the afternoon hobbyist.

For as long as I can remember, this blessed spot on the central California coast has represented freedom and boundless hopefulness. Its canyons snake through miles of uncharted dreams. The very mystery of creation astounds us at every turn and provides a constant reminder that each new day holds the promise of wonder. In some sense, it is no different from any beautiful place, just more so.

It is a haunting presence and will always be a place of the heart for me.

Jury Duty: The Wright Way

If there is one dreaded mail delivery for almost everyone I know, it has to be the ubiquitous jury duty notice. Why is that? This piece of paper seems to be the grand equalizer for professionals and the working class alike. It matters not how many degrees you have. You go. It is unfortunate that the thought of participating in a system designed to provide justice should be so distasteful. I have come to the conclusion that our resistance has little to do with the actual experience and everything to do with demands suggesting "involuntary servitude." After all, we are forced to alter our schedules and lose pay, and we have very little, if any, say in the matter. It feels somehow like coercion, and that never feels very good. For business owners, there is no making up for lost time; for employees, it is still time away. But we go nonetheless, kicking and screaming.

That is exactly what I did one recent December day when I knew it was zero hour and there was no more pushing the summons down the road. That being said, if one is to go kicking and screaming, better to go to a renowned futuristic landmark nestled among the Marin hills in Northern California than just about anywhere else.

The Marin County Civic Center is Frank Lloyd Wright's only completed government building, which he did not get to see before he died. The building is built on 140 acres, gracing the surrounding countryside with its beige earth tones, multiple archways, California blue sky roof, and 172-foot gold spire. Now why wouldn't anything be possible in a place like this? Is this not a perfect spot for a courtroom? If you are a Marin County resident, as I am, you are summoned to this location to perform your civic responsibility, although I never made it beyond the meet-and-greet morning coffee session where we gathered with identification in tow waiting for the verdict: to be chosen or to go home. And only in Marin County would the coffee in the civic center cafeteria be gourmet!

The civic center was the architect's 770th commission. One might think that by that time he would have lost his luster. Not so. The elongated serpentine building curves gracefully around, repeating a circular motif throughout. There is a skylighted planted atrium, as well as terrazzo floors and walkways. The feeling is one of open space with constant light overhead. Legend has it that Frank Lloyd Wright took his time and drove to the southernmost hill in the area to ponder the design. It was his intent to create an organic structure that would reflect the vast pastoral splendor of the Marin County landscape. In his own words, "We know that the good building is not the one that hurts the landscape, but is one that makes the landscape more beautiful than it was before the building was built." He succeeded and then some.

The Hall of Justice houses the civil and criminal courtrooms, which are designed in the round and have since been used as a model for courtrooms around the world. I, among many others, was directed to the jurors' holding pen. Occasionally, we would take walks around the perimeter of the building as we waited for word of our fate. No one seemed to mind as the hours dragged on. Ultimately, most of us were dismissed and never made it to the deeper recesses of the building. Unfortunately, I never got to see the courtrooms. But somehow the backdrop of this iconic space mitigated the imposition of being there. It was simply a moment in time—another day, but one spent in unique surroundings—amid the fantasies of a genius who somehow knew just how to stir our souls and still our restlessness.

Next time I receive my jury duty notice, I might just think differently about it.

Capri Close to Home

Whether it's images of vacationing Roman emperors or just the lure of escape, Italy's isle of Capri is everyone's fantasy. Capri, with its jagged cliffs swooping into eternity, sits above the Bay of Naples. But another Capri can be found a short distance from San Francisco, in Belvedere, overlooking the bay. This paradise is known as Corinthian Island. Although Corinthian is not really an island—rather more of a winding hill—and it has no hotels or amusements, only residences dotting the road, it is a sublime spot to grab a few stolen moments. This is the stuff of poets and princes: a flowered hillside rising toward heaven, persimmon palaces cast in shadows of late afternoon gold, yachts punctuating turquoise waters below. Just on the tip, hanging over the bay, is a bench welcoming weary visitors. Sometimes we don't have to look very far for enchantment.

CAPRI FAR FROM HOME

Over six thousand miles from California—America's Mediterranean, where I live—is Italy's isle of Capri. The island is named after the Greek "kapriae," which means "island of wild goats." Perhaps it got its name because it was thought that only wild goats could navigate the challenging terrain with ease. But the many visitors who populate the island also navigate with ease, so much so that, like Somerset Maugham's protagonist in *The Lotus Eaters*, many want to give up everything and stay for the rest of their lives. I know I did. There is just something about the atmosphere of the place.

On a recent June day, I saw Capri awash with color. As I descended a craggy path to the sea fringed with ancient ice-cream–colored villas with the mythical faraglioni rocks in the distance under a benevolent blue sky and the melodious sing-song of conversation wafting through the air, I knew I would always return. Capri may be far from home, but it has one thing Capri close to home does not: Italy.

SAMPLING PARADISE IN A CUP IN KAUAI, HAWAII

Picture this: you're sitting under a gazebo in Kauai with lush, emerald hills surrounding you, gentle breezes tickling your skin, and no sounds other than a palm rustling or a chicken or two strutting by. In this land of morning mists and afternoon rainbows, tongue-tingling sugarcane and succulent pineapple, it seems impossible to find one sublime moment surpassing the rest. Until you reach for your banana frostie, and then you know you have found it. Banana Joe's, a roadside fruit stand, is home to the banana frostie; it is a frothy concoction of naked bananas, the color of sun, with absolutely nothing added. The bananas are whipped to oblivion in a juicer. The feeling of the frostie gently gliding down your throat as you sit in this tropical Shangri-la is like nothing else. This velvety elixir is as seductive as the island itself—pure bliss. You think, *even paradise can't be this good.*

THINGS

We don't see things as they are, we see things as we are.

—Anais Nin

Radio Days

"Break a leg" they say. That's code in the trade for "have great success!" And that was the plan when I first embarked upon my radio career. It was a low-wattage one indeed in comparison to that of a national correspondent, but it certainly did create a buzz at dinner parties. Who have you interviewed? Who was your favorite?

My stint as a public affairs host at National Public Radio's flagship New York station WNYC and the local NBC stations in New York, WNBC and WYNY, lasted ten years until NBC sold its local radio outlets. The evolution of those radio days can be traced to a blend of both strategy and serendipity. After coming down from a relentless siege of unemployment as an entertainment publicist and a dose of torturous family health issues, an article in *Variety*, the entertainment bible, sparked a thought: WNYC, the station funded by New York City for over a century, was fundraising and needed help. It was looking for corporate and community support. Why not volunteer? I did exactly that and was welcomed with open arms. I offered promotional expertise from my publicist background, which was instantly translated into the creation of on-air radio spots. The task involved conceptualizing and implementing a blend of text and music that would seduce listeners into flicking their radio dial to the desired frequency. My first such project heralded an upcoming Phil Ochs concert commemorating his death. My opening line was Och's signature song. I remembered standing before my overworked program director, my hands trembling, as the tape began: "There but for fortune Phil Ochs might have continued on." I watched him percolate as the verbal images melded with the music. I knew I had chipped some bone!

The first time I heard my labor of love on the air, pure elation swept over me. I was hooked. So addictive was this newfound power that I was determined to make certain that my mentor's faith in me would not be shaken. The sweet little audio teasers reverberated through my head in shower stalls, on buses—just about everywhere—and would have sustained me indefinitely, even without pay. But then came the offer I could not refuse. "Have you ever thought of doing a show?" I hadn't really, but until the next morning, of course, I thought of nothing else! I could even hear it—a chatty intro, maybe some mellow Chuck Mangione music fading under my voice, and, of course, some snappy conversation. This was the birth of *New York Works*.

The WNYC station was the arts, culture, and community voice of New York—the jewel of National Public Radio's crown. *New York Works* was reflective of that mission. Although all the station hosts were volunteers, much to my delight, I was placed on the payroll and performed a variety of jobs at the station. As well as hosting and producing shows, my jobs ranged from programming to preparing financial reports—a task that would have been better left to just about anyone else. On my weekly program, luminaries, industry leaders, and a wide range of working stiffs shared their journeys across the intersection of work and life. Later, when I went on to ply my trade at NBC's local stations, WNBC and WYNY, my program morphed into *On the Job*, which presented arts and entertainment profiles as well as every conceivable gig out there from psychics and circus clowns to professors and poets. I wanted to know how work happened and about the satisfaction or lack thereof that it inspired. I was particularly enthralled with the chatty, inquisitive thirty-minute format. But in commercial radio, unlike WNYC, everything moved fast. Convinced that most listeners had the attention span of a flea, management soon asked that I reformat the show into brief segments with several guests and local job listings. I kicked and screamed, but I well understood that those were the new rules. If I wished to remain at the station, they were nonnegotiable.

The parade that marched through the studio was eclectic indeed. My first ever show was populated by two women representing alternate art perspectives. After myriad meetings before our scheduled taping, talk was lively, provocative, and flowed easily. I was psyched. Somehow on D-day, just about the time the first question was thrown out, one of the guests completely froze. Silence—complete silence. The sound of it was thunderous. I tried again. In jumped the second guest, who had suddenly developed a speech impediment! Only guttural sounds emerged in short, labored cadences. Of course, I was not flying high myself, as it was my debut show. My rookie radio persona descended on the scene like a vulture, swooping down over these two, feeding on whatever nutrients were there to save my own neck! Kudos went to my dear editor friend back in the studio, who cut this first wonder to smithereens but was somehow able to salvage a show.

Years down the road, when musical composer Jule Styne appeared on the program and did not stop singing his own compositions, I kept thinking how far I had come. Those gals from the first show could not start; he could not stop! And then there was the famed Liberace, adorned in pastel polyester, heavy metal medallion around his neck, hair impeccably coiffed, oozing irresistible charm and self-assurance. There was an unmistakable pride he had in simply being who he was—the consummate showman and ultimate gentleman, right down to his sequined shoes. When he sadly passed away a short time after the show aired, the program ran as a prime-time special—an honor indeed. And then there was the Ringling Bros lion tamer, draped in gray flannel. He looked more like Madison Avenue than Madison Square Garden—talk about stressful jobs! And I still remember when Joey Adams, the Borscht

Belt comedian tagged "the fastest joke teller in the East," pranced into the studio with enough attitude to burn more than a few bridges. He was not in much of a joking mood that day. After he refused to comply with standard operating procedure, I ushered him out, only to witness his return moments later, apology in tow.

The Picasso family was also well represented, with both Paloma and Françoise Gilot on separate shows. Paloma exhibited a great generosity of spirit; her mother, Françoise, less so when she refused to discuss her artistic relationship with Picasso, the very topic agreed upon for the show when she was initially invited. Nobel Laureate Isaac Bashevis Singer regaled the audience with his stories. When he graciously inscribed a book in my name, it read: "To Roberta Bole." Another great guest was Judy Collins, a true star, gracious and giving. I had the privilege of interviewing her twice. And let's not forget the appearance of the grand Swedish actress Viveca Lindfors, who richly came to life for thirty minutes only to discover that the technician had inadvertently neglected to record the program.

I had the good fortune of having so many talented and renowned guests. When people inquired what I did to gather such an impressive array of stars on my local show, I simply answered, "I asked them." Each personality brought sweetness, sharpness, style, and wisdom to the program. A great fortune teller who appeared in full business dress, when asked, "Can you make any money doing this?" Wisely replied, "it depends how you see yourself."

I never forgot that line. It resonated across the board and taught me a great deal about presentation and perception. I learned something of value each and every week. Everyone brought something different to the table; all of it was a great adventure that I never took for granted.

I count my radio days among my many blessings. Today, my archive remains intact, albeit somewhat dusty. Although much time has passed, those many voices can still be heard with perfect clarity through the din of the years.

Nobody Sends Letters Anymore

iPhone, YouTube. What's sweeter than a tweet?

It's July 2010, and I'm sticking with the basics: my dumb phone—a flip top—and my garden variety laptop. No smart phones for me. Unless they make dinner, who needs them? My able fingers can still do the walking. Finding everything at the touch of a button can feel somehow numbing. My cell phone is a savior for logistics, scheduling, and, of course, emergencies, but not for meandering conversation. In fact, when I feel one coming and my ear begins to heat up, I nip it in the bud immediately by signing off and promising to reconnect on my land line at home. While there is no conclusive evidence that cell phone radiation is cancer causing, such talk is off-putting as far as I am concerned. The jury is still out. For me, it is as good an excuse as any to keep my use to a minimum.

Whenever I leave home, I prefer to travel light. A wondrous world is spinning around me. What is the need for a few "apps" or the clicking of some keys to uncover yet another one? Get with the program, you say; the horse and buggy has been replaced by the car. But I can't help but wonder how we ever survived—and in some cases thrived—without these techno toys? We were able to solve problems in a pinch; we were also less likely to arrive late for appointments when we did not have a phone available for last-minute damage control. And there was never a time when we would be lunching with someone while heeding the siren call of another with only a perfunctory "Sorry, I must take this. I'll be just a minute." These are famous last words indeed, as idle chitchat takes hold and our lunch partner begins to wonder why we had not chosen to lunch with the caller instead.

We all have our stellar cellular moments. I remember being seated in a small wedding chapel waiting for the bride to make her appearance when suddenly the silence was broken by the booming sounds of a baritone in the back. This moment was only eclipsed by my neighbor in a ladies room stall chattering about prurient matters, all accompanied by the roar of a flush. And do we really need to hear a cacophony of voices heralding arrival whenever a plane touches down?

But despite the seductive convenience of it all, there are times when even our cell phones are just too intimate, and so we gaze at the ubiquitous computer screen. Texting, tweeting, and e-mails are fine. I must confess that there are moments when I like ducking one-on-one interactions as much as the next gal, and these pathways can lead to bliss. They are clean, fast, and efficient, and they cut right to the chase. But please, let's skip them for extravagant moments of joy, sadness, gratitude, or celebration. For those occasions, we still have our phones—or perhaps even letters! How about letters? No one sends letters anymore! But you must admit, there is something magical about retrieving that crisp little envelope in the mail, the one that has taken its time traveling across the street or over the miles. We take our time to read it and respond, not merely to react. There is a difference. A response happens over time and is reflective; a reaction is immediate and reflexive. Therein lies the difference.

What about social networks? Where do they fit in? It feels as if my worst nightmare—that the world will become one giant cocktail party—has come to pass. Social networks have introduced a universe in which strangers become "friends"—a universe in which we are out there for all to see, through moments of merriment as well as mourning. For the small pleasure of peeking behind otherwise closed doors, we pay the price of broken hearts, spirits, and egos when we feel we don't measure up to the slick, enviable lives of "friends" as they portray themselves for our viewing. But friendship—the old-fashioned kind—knows no shortcut. Authentic connection is a slow process that moves in increments of intimacy and trust. Waiting for it to evolve naturally can feel like waiting for water to boil. It takes time and patience. But it is the only way I know to be "friended" or to "friend" in the truest sense.

Don't get me wrong, I have no beef with staying in touch. I welcome social connection every chance I get, but are we talking about connection here or just a quick fix for our collective ennui? Are we merely operating on impulses to maximize every opportunity to gossip, gab, and gawk? To be engaged at all times, anywhere and everywhere, is to turn our lives into a mere reality show and not to be engaged at all.

Hair

For more years than I care to remember, like most women, I have made the grooming of my hair a fairly regular activity in my life. When I am not bent over the sink applying, combing, blowing, teasing, crunching, curling, or straightening, I am visiting a salon where someone else is doing these things for me—for a price, of course. It can be a delightful pampering experience, but it can also turn into a nightmare. It has actually occurred to me many times over the years that the true power brokers of the world do not inhabit Wall Street. They are not financiers or corporate raiders; they do not deal with hedge funds. They deal with hair! Let's face it—there is no one better positioned to ruin our sense of well-being than our hairdressers. We trust them, after all; they cradle our heads in their hands as their deft fingers knead our delicate strands into permanent waves of nourishment. When the warm towel gets wrapped around us, once again we are six and it is bath time. From the moment we disrobe and adorn ourselves in salon garb, the whole experience is almost primal. No wonder the vulnerability meter goes way up. Not to mention the all-important outcome—how our hair looks! Perhaps that is why our confidence can be so easily ruptured in the space of a few hours. All at once we find ourselves at the mercy of some clueless colorist or some unstylish stylist who sees auburn as crimson and a little trim as a scalping, try as we may to communicate otherwise. Clearly, after the deed is done and the guilty party exhibits no remorse, it is time to assert our rights. But we are children in the midst of all-too-powerful authority figures, and so instead we parade around the salon in our faded gray gowns past others with gobs of goo, listening as some employee who was not responsible for the demise of our good looks effusively compliments us on the very hairdo we so abhor. Is this some kind of conspiracy? We are then forced to grease the palms of all on this chain of command on our way out, for we might need to return to have our train wreck of a hairdo corrected. And so we abscond with the goods on our head and beat a hasty retreat back to our sinks at home to undo everything that was done. If we do return to have our tresses redressed, we must endure the humiliation of walking again past a bevy of workers who, if eyes could talk, would be saying, "Who does that diva think she is? She won't look any different anyway."

But a hair salon should always be client friendly, you say—an environment in which a contract is honored and the customer is always right. *Wrong*! Perhaps we the clients must take responsibility for some of this poor communication. All too often, I have seen people acting with unnecessary deference, ignoring the fact that they are the recipients of a service for which they are paying. In the final analysis, this is a business arrangement, nothing more. In any other such arrangement, we would not think twice about fully asserting our needs and following through if they were not met. What exactly is the intimidation here? Why do we feel so tempted to disappear into the sunset or buy a new hat to conceal the damage instead of expecting and demanding that the job be completed to our satisfaction? Is this even about hair? It seems to resemble a power play more than anything else. After all, nothing is quite as personal as our self image and the way we choose to present ourselves. To put our carefully orchestrated image in the hands of strangers who may or may not understand us, assuming they even care, is placing us on shaky ground. No wonder we feel vulnerable and behave in kind.

And just think about it—who among us has not secretly yearned to flatten the pompadour of the guy in front of us in the movie line or brighten the mousy curls on the gal standing alongside him—and to get paid for it, no less! Hairdressers get to do this every day! Besides, this hair thing is not an exact science. At best, it is an art. Most of the time, it is a job. In some cases, it might even be more fitting to have our hairdressers pay us for the opportunity to test some pretty extravagant fantasies on our heads.

Why should all this matter anyway? Isn't what's in our head what is important, not what is on it? Ah yes, but unless our god-given strands are perfected to our liking, we fear that no one will bother to discover what is in our heads. So the routine goes and will continue as long as there is hair and there are salons. Our ultimate goal, of course, is to appear as if little or no effort or expense was involved in achieving our impeccably groomed hair. And let's face it—it really does behoove us to remain on the best of terms with our hairdressers. As we have been repeatedly reminded, it is only they who know for sure.

Picking Up Signals

I had my first brush with the power of communication when I was seven. It happened at the cosmetics counter of my local drugstore while I was shopping with my mom. I saw a big, bold, brash woman with jewels glistening on her wrists, neck, and ankles. I was transfixed. But it was her hair that was her crowning glory—a mound of crimson curls. I had not seen hair like that before; it was on fire. I looked long and hard without diverting my gaze. She looked back. Her eyes were fixed on me; her lips pursed in a cold smirk. I responded with unabashed innocence and said, "I love your beautiful red hair. How do you comb it?"

We were instant comrades. I watched that woman melt before my very eyes. I simply did what was instinctively right. Everything about her face spoke to me; she would not be mocked. As soon as I assured her that I was expressing approval and not criticism, any and all resentment was diffused, and a potentially contentious situation was averted.

We cannot not communicate! There is no interaction in which communication, verbal or otherwise, does not play a part. When we interface with another, what we wear, how we touch, how we use space and time, and, of course, what we say affects our impressions, future thoughts, decisions—you name it. Studies have determined that nonverbal behaviors account for 65 to 93 percent of the total meaning of a communication message. When verbal and nonverbal communication do not match (such as saying "sure I love you" as you are grimacing), we go with the nonverbal every time. This is where our true feelings live! Otherwise, why would we so often hear "It is not what you say but how you say it?"

It is possible to speak volumes through gestures and body language. I remember riding a bus and watching the driver yawn, stretch, and grunt every few seconds. He could only have been saying one of two things: "I am tired" or "I am bored," neither of which makes the riders of that bus feel very good about who is at the controls. And haven't we all had the experience of waiting in miserably cold or rainy conditions at a bus stop only to see the bus parked with the driver warmly tucked in his seat ignoring the masses waiting outside. He need not say a word—he is saying a great deal!

Daily life is ripe with communication cues, but do we take them? Consider dining out. One would assume good food + attractive décor= a good experience. Not so. In a Zagat survey several years ago, what over forty percent of respondents complained most about was the service— and service, after all, is about communication, isn't it? It begins before we even enter the restaurant, when we are making a reservation over the phone. If we are rushed, patronized, or put indefinitely on hold, then subliminally if not consciously, we are primed for disappointment. When we arrive at the restaurant only to be whisked away to a table in the boondocks, it gets progressively worse. Our server then appears, introducing him or herself, reciting the specials, and disappearing while we contemplate our choices. The server's return would be a good time to read the table rather than merely take the order. Who are these diners and what are they looking for? Are they here for status, food, or entertainment? How quickly do they want the meal to progress, and how sophisticated are they about the food and wine?

But how can waitstaff know these things? Easy. Pay attention; the cues are not hard to miss. For example: you are nestled in a quiet corner, just the two of you, arms intertwined, lost in intimate conversation, only to be interrupted multiple times by your server inquiring if everything is okay. Just look and listen: smiles, soft voices, embraces, and animated conversation all point to okay. The diners might even be more okay if some small modicum of privacy were granted. How obvious, and yet how elusive.

As the meal draws to a close, one last intervention is observed: the sweeping away of the plate. No matter that a few small morsels still lurk there, it must be seized immediately. But not before we hear those all-too-familiar words, "Still working?" Even worse, I have actually heard "Still chewing?" Rest assured that if I ever run a restaurant, anyone who utters "Still working?" will not be, at least not for me.

So what is a respectable diner to do? Is there recourse? How do we respond? At the end of the day, there remains one powerful tool in our communication arsenal. Yep, you guessed it: the tip! That may just be our last-ditch effort to answer that persistent question, "Is everything okay?"

TEACHABLE MOMENTS

It is becoming increasingly difficult to imagine that several decades ago, generations of college-educated women seeking careers looked to teaching as their one ticket to the dance. And yet many of us opted not to go that route. Elementary education was a highly popular major when I was in school; college-level teaching was something else again. It required a graduate degree, which was a time consuming proposition that would only delay homemaking and child rearing—which was, of course, our raison d'être. Few of us messed with the mission. Teaching certainly didn't resonate for me. College teaching was the province of the tweedy set. Elementary school teaching was even less of a calling, as it reeked of "babysitting" large groups of six year olds and seemed to demand endless patience and little creativity—or so I thought. How ignorant I was! I set out for random job interviews for everything from publicity to journalism, leather briefcase holding breath mints and the newspaper in tow. I was repeatedly asked: "What can you do?" I was horrified. I could read, after all, even think on a good day, and sometimes communicate those thoughts with a fair degree of aplomb. Perfect credentials for a teacher.

What I would actually do with my degree in English literature was of less consequence than what I would not do. Only years into middle adulthood did it ever occur to me that teaching could be a course to follow. Teaching, I came to see, is the best chance we have to be proactive in shaping the world. To attempt to excite and develop young minds is no small thing. Curiously, after a variety of gigs, one day I found myself on a trajectory that led to graduate school and ultimately to college teaching. I was blessed to teach at New York University, one of the finest, most prestigious universities in the nation, in the company of fifty savvy, curious post-adolescents every Tuesday and Thursday for seventeen years. They would challenge my ever-so-slick persona with answers to questions I didn't even have. As I was a refugee from radio, one of my classes was on public speaking. This discipline left me with no room to wither and die, as we are all wont to do from time to time; I was the public speaking teacher, after all. Most days, I was up to the task and gave myself the proverbial pat on the back. But there were others when I was less so; all I had to do was read the faces of the class to see exactly where I stood. Like any veteran performer, I was only as good as my audience, and my audience was top-notch. Those kids were my laboratory.

At home in the evening, preparing exercises or reading speeches, I would sometimes get weary. When I hit the classroom the next morning, the tedium would instantly abate. Refreshed and invigorated, I knew that I was on board for the job as long as they would have me. All I needed to confirm the magic was one head vigorously nodding in agreement, one reluctant warrior who at the beginning of the term would rather die than speak, waving furiously to go first by the last class, or one note years later saying, "Professor Cole—you changed my life."

Yet a good teacher is always hanging on the precipice of uncertainty. Do they get it? How can I help them to feel both comfortable and empowered? Sometimes all it took to know if I was even on the right track was one student. A "master of the universe" business school student looking to show off comes to mind. During a free choice speech assignment, he decided to sing the praises of pass/fail classes and to disclose, against university guidelines, that he was a pass/fail student. Spewing arrogance, he insisted that taking a class pass/fail enabled him to stay at the bar the night before instead of being at home preparing. I listened intently. As I looked around the class, I noticed some eye rolling among his classmates. I allowed the speech and critiques to proceed. I later met with the student in my office, away from his small circle of comrades, and asked him if it was his intention to trash the class. Surely he understood that to do so would be to trash his education as well. I inquired why he would want to do that, and I then assured him that the pass/fail option was indeed working; with this sort of behavior, he would surely fail.

During subsequent classes, he wore his newfound dignity like a fine suit. By the end of the semester, I was certain not only that he would pass the class but also that he exuded a different sense of self. In my interpersonal communication class, I required substantial term papers as part of the grade. The papers were long, and I read them multiple times. I was blown away by the breadth and depth of some of them. When specific students were recruited to read them aloud, if they were comfortable doing so, I sensed a bonding among the rest of the class. Learning flowed in all directions.

And then there were those teacher evaluations at the end of the semester. Students were asked to provide numerical ratings for specific points: teacher availability, interest, and clarity of material as well as gratuitous comments if desired. I was ushered out of the room, and a student would collect the forms and bring them to my department. After the grading period was over, I would get to read them. Ever since I have been away from teaching, students have generated more electronic teacher evaluations. As a matter of fact, they have become quite widespread, which I feel is unfortunate. These are ostensibly to inform and protect students from the onslaught of poor teachers, but I suspect that in far too many cases, something else is going on. Teaching is certainly subjective and should not be a popularity contest. In the case of nontenured teachers, grade inflation has become an epidemic, because sadly too many of these teachers fall prey to the pressure of keeping their jobs at all costs. Anything fostering continuation of the contract between teachers and students to give good grades in exchange for good reviews must be discouraged.

Public denouncement of a teacher is inappropriate and unnecessary; it can easily become sport under the right fraternity or sorority house conditions. Teachers must retain their conviction that a grade is earned, not given, and that accolades are only meaningful when they stem from true academic integrity. Evaluations can sting. Curiously, no matter how many positive ones are garnered, we look at the few negative ones and agonize. Perhaps that is not a bad thing if it keeps teachers fresh. I remember reading the evaluations after the term was over and smiling as I read the first: "This is the best teacher I ever had." It was immediately followed by the next review declaring, "This is the worst teacher I ever had."

Recently, *New York Times* columnist David Brooks noted that "94 percent of college professors believe they have above-average teaching skills." I was comforted to see that these professors evaluated themselves as above average and not as excellent. Within that margin between above average and excellent, there are still miles to travel. That is not a bad thing.

The smartest, most engaged students offer tremendous dynamism, and what better platform is there for helping to develop these fertile minds than teaching? Although I left teaching some four years ago when I relocated to the West Coast, I still try to incorporate some of the skills and wisdom I acquired from those many fertile minds in every endeavor in my current life. I loved every minute of teaching. There is no more rewarding way to spend one's time.

A Certain Necessary Thing

That year, I was twenty-six and restless. I needed a place that would welcome my eager body leaning toward freedom. I had an enviable job that I didn't want to leave, but I did want to go. I caught the travel bug on a short honeymoon in Europe, and I wanted more.

It was my fourth year as a publicist with United Artists, a major film company, but in some ways it was the winter of my discontent. I met movie stars, attended film screenings, wrote press releases, and conversed with anyone who would listen in a manner more suited to a philosophy major than a film publicist. "The film was Kafkaesque," I would hear myself say, feet pointing down from my cluttered metal desk, suspended over the freshly carpeted floor below. I had a cork wall, a secretary, and an inflated notion of what was possible. Pressing my nose against the glass of the rich and famous made me think that if life could be this good, it could be even better. I aimed to find out.

Nights were spent writhing around the wrinkled mass that was my bed. My husband, out of sheer desperation, encouraged my arrival at a decision: to stay at my job, or to bolt? I wanted a six-month leave of absence, but what I was offered was not even close.

"Take six weeks," my department head said. "You can see everything and still have your job."

But it wasn't about seeing everything, it was about living something. A tough call for a kid who had caught the brass ring.

It was only a concrete slab, this place I discovered in a small West Village square in lower Manhattan, hardly the seat of deep thought. After many months of Sundays, I christened it "Decision Park." For it was there in that spot that my fate was ultimately decided. I weighed the options, which were far too heady for someone in her third decade of life: to quit my job, or to continue in the direction of the executive dining room? I wasn't alone in Decision Park. There were other great thinkers—men with five o'clock shadows approaching midnight, too tired for chess, and their female counterparts, long retired from their domestic heydays, draped in robes that had lined the racks of local thrift shops. For my part, jeans with a fresh crease down the center, a ribbed turtleneck, and an acceptably rugged leather jacket were just fine.

Pictures flashed in front of me with dizzying persistence—images of a life light years away from Broadway's watering holes, where wine poured like water on the company tab. I could taste my newly imagined freedom but could not imagine my unemployment nightmare—the interminable days in front of a silent telephone at journey's end if I turned down my employer's benevolent offer. I could only feel the speed of the silvery serpentine caravan and see from its window the European countryside with its crusty colored houses, fields covered with a chartreuse glaze of daisies, and broad boulevards lined with wicker chairs surrounding sidewalk tables where talk was always animated. I wanted to stand before the Lego-like wonderlands of antiquity and exchange glances with strangers who had lived what I could not even dream. On Monday morning, in the corner office, the words "six months" left my lips with as much difficulty as glue pouring from a bottle. Next thing I knew, I stood in an airport terminal in a sweat, my entire body throbbing with anticipation. It was Bastille Day. My mother and I were on our way to France with some squeaky new Tourister bags, an air ticket, and the hope that I had not made a terrible mistake.

My husband was between gigs, and he planned to join me in a few weeks. At that point, my mother was planning to embark on her own journey. The months that followed contained the kind of rapture I had only imagined: wanderings through markets scented with cinnamon, ascents to white-frosted mountaintops, tavernas, trattorias, paradors, and pensiones, dusty old bull rings, turquoise harbors, and enough town squares to last a lifetime. The joy of total spontaneity was palpable, and it was only briefly interspersed with the tedium of finding a Laundromat, a shoe repair shop, and enough of the local currency lining our pockets to enable my husband and me to share a much coveted shower. That's how tight the budget was. Our days were unlike any we had experienced before. Towns that would have gone unnoticed back home held a magic that could only have been possible for twenty-somethings. We were intoxicated by the distant horizon that seemed far enough to stir our souls but close enough to be just within reach. How young we were.

Six months later to the day, I walked into the chill New York night with the exotic smells of my adventure still on my clothing, a silent telephone awaiting my return, and a certain necessary thing on my mind.

THE RULE OF COOL

Driving that little vintage sports car with the top down, skipping the overcoat when no one else does, wearing sunglasses when it's dark—what do they all have in common? Yep, they are all behaviors perceived as cool. But wait a minute. What does that mean? Doesn't it depend on where and who you are? And also on the time in which you are living—and, of course, on who's judging? The cool little car could at any time be eclipsed by the monstrous Hummer, and the scanty little shirt just might have to make way for the wearable blanket! Trends move fast and are hard to keep up with. And what is cool, anyway? Why are we so willing to be uncomfortable to achieve it? Have you ever seen motorcyclists adorned head to toe in black leather on summer's hottest day? Or tank tops and flip flops worn when fleece and boots would be more in keeping with the temperature? Why do we suffer the pain of tattooing or piercing? After all, when all is said and done, the very approval we are seeking may not even come to pass.

We do know for sure that cool is mutable and different for all of us. It can be based on attitude, appearance, or behavior; it can vary from culture to culture. But it is certainly thought to be a desirable commodity, perhaps because it almost always suggests membership in that great social club called acceptance—until, of course, it doesn't. Membership can mean friends, an inflated sense of well-being, and even wealth. The only problem is the ever-present difficulty of getting it right and the undue effort expended toward that goal. This quest can make us frustrated, tired, cold, and sick. It can even kill us.

Sadly, none of us is immune. I remember as a young girl doing constant battle with my mother over skirt length. In my view, it was just not cool to go ambling down the street with my skirt covering my knees. My mother disagreed. But there was a solution, as there always is. I simply wore it at the approved length until I was out the door. Once I was in what I thought was safe territory, I rolled it up to be acceptably cool. It never took very long before I would spy my mother coming in my direction and things would begin to heat up. The skirt was once again rolled down.

There is no single expression of cool. Ironically, the bearer of judgment must be cool to perceive it in another. But is that necessarily the same cool? And again, what exactly is cool? While it is a slang term in the English language, it is understood in other languages and is generally perceived as positive. It can also be used to suggest agreement, as in "I am cool with that," or to suggest emotional calmness during a storm. One thing is clear: no one wants to be "uncool," so we go back once again to reaffirm the hallmarks of cool. One problem: we cannot! Remember that Hummer? Maybe, just maybe, it has turned once again into a Mini Cooper or a Smart Car. And to confuse us even more, in today's jargon, hot is cool because it suggests attributes of attractiveness, which we all seek. Someone who is hot is also usually cool. So what to do? Are we striving for hot or cool, or are they the same?

And just how far will we go? Take smoking for example: multitudes of us, including myself, have taken paper housing particles of tobacco, inhaled it, and then blown smoke out When we were not engaging in this ridiculous act, we were simply wearing the cigarettes like status jewelry, either in our hand, above our ear, or peeking out from the top of our back pocket. As teenagers, we felt naked without them. Jazz musicians and movie stars epitomized sophistication as they cradled drinks and puffed on cigarettes or the more phallic version—the cigar—which not only got smoked but also chewed. And pipes, of course, which somehow made us look professorial and grandfatherly. Great philosophers and lovers throughout history have delivered exit lines shrouded in billowing clouds of smoke. For rebels, even without causes, a cigarette was a badge of irreverence, a true mark of distinction. But no more. Now we know they kill—very uncool. But still, baseball stars, our national heroes, chew the stuff.

Another mark of cool is the way we like to perceive ourselves as indestructible. No need for protection. Why wear a helmet? That is for wimps. If you set out to weather the storms without protection and you emerge intact, well then, you must surely be cool. But again, think how uncool you will be if you do not emerge intact. Many fatal accidents could be prevented if cool did not rule. Is wearing a seatbelt cool? You bet your life.

We tend to think of adolescence as the time when cool rules. But certainly the Beat generation as they aged, as well as many baby boomers, proved that not to be the case. We still gyrate over aging rock bands whose persona has changed very little. Well into old age, it is possible to be governed by cool, if not through behavior then through appearance or language.

Historically, films have mirrored the habits of a culture and in many instances defined and shaped coolness. Classic lines from movies resonate for generations. But one line, one shred of wisdom, from a film called *Almost Famous* sticks with me. After we follow the young protagonist in his relentless quest for cool, we share the film's epiphany through the following line, delivered by one of the characters: "The only true currency in this bankrupt world is what we share with someone else when we are uncool."

Wow! Wouldn't it be liberating if we could actually see not being cool as having value? We might even experience an enviable freedom from chasing social acceptance. What would happen if we were truly able to define cool for ourselves and it was whatever we were? What if our own distinctiveness and specialness could be enough?

How "cool" would that be?

THE SHORT LIST

Maybe it's just me, but does anyone speak in full sentences anymore? Have we become a culture that has a need to abbreviate everything? Yes, there were always abbreviations—phone, TV—but nowadays, substituting initials for the shortest possible sentences seems to have taken on a life of its own. It gives one pause when we hear one of history's most bloodcurdling events referred to by a mere two numbers: 9/11. Is it too much effort to eke out the words "September eleventh?" Somehow the magnitude of the event seems to call for a more substantial means of referencing it; 9/11 is way too casual and somehow strikes a chord of disrespect. There is a certain solemnity that is called for here; and for me the sound of those two numbers gives the occasion short shrift.

But letters and words are arbitrary—they are mere symbols and are discretionary, after all. The problem, assuming there is one, lies in the affective connotation. Language has its own way of speaking. Our perceptions are filtered through symbols. When we name or label something in one way or another, our thought process is impacted. Thus we see an object or an event in a particular way as a result of the language we use to describe it. I did not invent this thinking. Linguist Benjamin Whorf and anthropologist Edward Sapir hypothesized that our perception of reality is determined by our thought processes and that our thought processes are limited by our language. So what's with the abbreviations? I wonder if this fast food of language simply makes the reality a little easier to digest—or makes horrific events seem a bit more familiar and comfortable.

Take for example, the initials used for a plethora of diseases. Not a day goes by when we do not see some medication advertised on TV (not television!) Promoted to heal COPD, ADD, ADHD, EDD, RA, GERD, or PMS. What's going on here? Yes, there were always ALS, MS, and TB, but it seems we now have enlisted an entire alphabet for just about everything to help make the medicine go down. Are these diseases and afflictions minimized in our perception by reducing them to a few benign initials? I'll go a step further: do we create an affliction by providing a few short initials to label it?

Technology, of course, has provided us with a language all its own. When mobile phones first hit the market, they were referred to as cellular telephones. They rapidly became cell phones, and now they are cells—"Call me on my cell." What will they think of next? No wonder there is talk of e-mail becoming obsolete in favor of texting and tweeting. Far less effort is expended when we text or tweet. If we can speak in short, clipped code, why bother doing anything else? There was a time when we spoke of the medium being the message. I'm wondering, have we come full circle? Is the message now the medium? Nowadays you cannot even go into a government office without hearing the ubiquitous question wafting through the open cubicles: What's your "social?" Is that a sexually transmitted disease (excuse me, STD) or does it refer to our social security numbers? If the latter, why not just say so?

Is communication being reduced to one giant abbreviation? If so, why bother at all?

Pancakes on Monday

"Butter girl," I would hear as we circled the tangerine walls of the kitchen in our first tiny New York apartment, preparing the week's reward. It was Sunday, and that meant hotcakes, dripping with an irresistible golden sweetness. Who knew or cared about calories or cholesterol? We were young newlyweds; we were indestructible. Other mornings were spent heeding the shrill sound of the alarm, but not Sunday. Sunday was for luxuriating, for wearing warm, colorful robes and flopping down on squeaky new furniture. The Second Avenue landscape outside our window would engage us on other days, but Sunday was the period at the end of the sentence. It deserved to be taken seriously.

My husband Jeff would pour the gooey batter from a perfectly glazed bowl—probably received as a wedding gift—into a frying pan. At the command of "butter girl," I would garnish the freshly formed mountains of dough layered on top of one another with appropriately large slabs of butter. It doesn't get much better! We would then pile the sink sky-high with dishes while we recovered from this divine indulgence. Pleasures were many back then, but they had their place and did not often spill into the deferred gratification program we had bought into. Curiously, during those years when we had all the time in the world, we actually had very little time at all. Fast forward a couple of decades. Time is plentiful, but only in the short term. The days are long, but the years ahead are not.

I try to remember what our notions of retirement were initially. I guess it was something between a gold watch and an endless stream of weekends. Regardless, its seductiveness persisted. Our daughter was grown, and for Jeff, who had spent the bulk of his years suited and ever ready for the kill, fantasies of uninterrupted leisure were attractive to say the least. Jeff was a lawyer, and for a lawyer practicing with a fairly large prestigious law firm, one's life is not one's own. Any day and any time of day was open season for clients to have their way with him. I can remember many dinners and vacations abruptly cut short by the sound of a ringing telephone. What Jeff had thought would be the gentlemanly practice of law morphed into what seemed to be constant enslavement. Boundaries were always stretched; more often than not, they were broken. The pervading attitude was "If I don't service this client, someone else will." Curiously, when we were young and Jeff was new at his game, time off was sacred. A three-week uninterrupted vacation was commonplace. It wasn't until he became a senior partner that he began to feel like an indentured servant.

I followed a very different course, working first as a publicist in the entertainment industry, later in broadcasting as a host and producer of my own show, and finally in academia as an adjunct professor. In comparison to Jeff, demands on my time were few. While my relatively flexible schedule provided the opportunity for me to work out of a home office much of the time, the lure of glamour and creativity still had the same pull. That pull kept me out there and in the same quicksand as Jeff. We both thought of retirement as an end instead of a beginning. Through the years, Jeff's worn leather briefcase was an appendage—a part of his body. It took many stresses and even illness to move that briefcase into the far reaches of a closet. For a long time, whenever the phone rang, there was an instantaneous fear that it would be some corporate upstart soliciting Jeff for what later appeared to be a contrived emergency. For me, quitting would conceivably mean the end to lively cocktail party chatter peppered with references to the prestigious celebrities I interviewed and the impressive teaching credentials suggested by my university affiliation.

The day finally came, but not until after we relocated to the San Francisco Bay Area from the East Coast. At that point, it took very little time for Jeff to ease into his new life; for me, the transition was almost immediate. The sturdy wrought-iron desk in Jeff's new home office quickly became a receptacle for reams of paper detailing local amusements: hikes, events, and the like. The small print at the bottom of the list outlined destinations like the cleaner and the grocery store, but such destinations were only to be given attention after the primary list was crossed off. Occasionally a road trip or a larger adventure would be planned; we would take many visits to the local Barnes & Noble for maps, tips, etc. In other words, half the fun was getting there! These trips also included frequent stops at the local candy outlet for a sweet, salty chocolate peanut butter confection just to confirm that we were on the right track!

I immediately embraced the new status of being a free agent who had climbed out on a limb to grab the fruit of a different experience. I rather liked that image. Now cocktail party chatter included wide-eyed envy of the midlife risks I had taken, putting me in the company of those sturdy souls willing to give up certain comfort and predictability for adventure. Funny how we get mileage out of different things at different times.

Though retirement life does not follow a predictable schedule, our mornings are usually spent in independent pursuits while afternoons generally mean joint activities, which can range from a toss of the ball at the local Bocce court to a hike along an ocean trail or exploration of a neighborhood in our recently adopted city. Does this sound too good to be true? Don't we all wonder if retirement will mean boredom? When friends who are still actively engaged in business as usual ask us if we are ever bored, we answer with a resounding no!

Is she for real, you ask? Here's the thing: *bored* is a word that suggests unrelenting weariness. Restless is more the issue. Are we ever restless? To adequately answer that question, one must first acknowledge that restlessness certainly rears its head at work, does it not? But somehow we forget; even the most repetitive, tedious chore at work becomes preferable in our minds to the terrifying prospect of unstructured time. So yes, we might feel restless. There are worse afflictions! But one of the great perks is the ability to let a day ramble. When we are asked "How are you?" It is no longer a perfunctory question. We actually have the time and inclination to respond. Gratuitous conversation thrives once again—not always a good thing, I admit!

The deal about retirement is that, just like so many life transitions, you can't define the experience until you actually own it. The texture and quality of it is ever changing depending on attitude, circumstance, and fortune, and by that I do not necessarily mean finances. The overriding thought that keeps coming back, though, is that there really is a terrific energy and power in the ability to reinvent, and reinventing is exactly what needs to happen. We must take the "tire" out of retire in order to seize this second chance to transform our lives. The resulting lifestyle may not be perfect, but it does hold the potential to infuse our later years with new sparkle and discovery. If a spouse or a partner is in the picture, it is also possible to mold your relationship into whatever this new time in life may present. Will you ever get on each other's nerves? Yes, but probably no more than you did before! As humans we have the uncanny ability to obsess over small details that obstruct harmony at any and all hours of the day. This tendency does not only exist and prosper during daytime hours, although it is true that more time spent together means a greater likelihood of quarrels. Yes, I want the heat off when he wants the heat on a little more often than I did when we were working—a small price!

Think of retirement as a stew. You throw in a little of this and a little of that and see what happens. Let it simmer and be prepared for something hearty and rich, if not always sublimely delicious. The true balance lies in remaining focused while allowing an openness to serendipity. And the good news is that for most of us, retirement may be the first real time we get to call the shots for ourselves. Weekends no longer hold their former power.

Now when Jeff calls out "butter girl," it may just be Monday!

www.ingramcontent.com/pod-product-compliance
Lightning Source LLC
Chambersburg PA
CBHW020240290526
45784CB00003B/1053